Musings from a Greek Village
PETER BARBER'S MUSINGS
BOOK ONE

PETER BARBER

Please note that this book is the original creation of the author. The author wrote and compiled it entirely without the use of any artificial intelligence.

USE OF THIS BOOK FOR AI TRAINING:

Without in any way limiting the author's and publisher's exclusive rights under copyright, any use of this publication to "train" generative artificial intelligence (AI) technologies to generate text is expressly prohibited. The author reserves all rights to license uses of this work for generative AI training and development of machine learning language models.

Copyright © 2023 Peter Barber

Formatted and published by Ant Press, 2023

Cover illustration by Charly Alex Fuller

ISBN: 978-1-916574-15-1 Paperback

ISBN: 978-1-916574-16-8 Hardback

ISBN: 978-1-916574-17-5 Large Print Paperback

ISBN: 978-1-916574-18-2 Large Print Hardback

All rights reserved.

No part of this book may be reproduced in any form or by any electronic or mechanical means, including information storage and retrieval systems, without written permission from the author, except for the use of brief quotations in a book review.

Contents

A brief introduction.	1

JANUARY

Greece is changing, but not my village.	5
Good morning and Happy New Year.	8
How Greek have I become?	11
It's snowing. Yes, in Greece.	14
Hooker or Hookah?	17
We older people should know our limits.	18
The eye.	21
In Greece, cats chase dogs.	24
Adventure with Avis	26
How Greece has changed!	29
Ok. I agree. It's Greek.	32
Alex in trouble (again).	35
Mosquitos are stupid.	38
Look into her eyes.	40
Writing about Greece.	42

FEBRUARY

Writing about Greece can be really dangerous.	47
Sore heads and Spam on the side	49
"The energy of the mind is the essence of life" – Aristotle	52
Am I sad or proud?	56
My famous wife.	59
Living in Greece. Know the rules.	62
"You don't like my food?"	65
It's Carnival time in Greece.	68
The sea is the way, they say.	71
The new Durrells? Perhaps not.	75

MARCH

The world's worst builders. (Part 1)	81
The world's worst builders. (Part 2)	84
A delicate operation. (Part 1)	88
A delicate operation. (Part 2)	91
Independence Day.	95
The wonderful traditions of my Greece.	96
Scary boat cover.	99

Some people feel sorry for me. 102
Greeks obey rules. (Eventually.) 105

APRIL

The weather warning. 111
Hissssss... 112
Just a little gardening. 114
Shopping in our Greek village. 116
The Greek sun is sneaky. 119
Beware!! In Greece, shopping can get you drunk. 122
The way home. 125
A lovely day in the village. 128
The incredible story of two Greek cats. 130
My wife isn't speaking today. 132
Good news! 134
Experience the real Greece. 137
Don't ask what's in it. (Part 1) 140
Don't ask what's in it. (Part 2) 143
A lovely day on my island. 146
Where have all the proper dogs gone? 149
Greece is changing. 151
Greek phrases, slogans, and profanities. 155
What a fabulous day in Greece! 157

MAY

Another hot day in our village	163
Octopus-flavoured doughnuts.	166
Lost in translation.	170
A simple story of life in my Greek village.	173
Dentist chairs and sticky cake windows.	175
Karpouzi – refreshes the parts other fruits cannot reach.	178
It's Eurovision Song Contest time again.	181
Saturday rant.	184
The Greek chef. Well, almost.	187
Remembering my other mother.	190
Relax, take your time. You're in Greece.	193
More fun in the Greek village.	196
The diet starts tomorrow, again.	200
A Parthenon on Our Roof.	203
Hammock wars.	207
Our local fruit supplier.	210
Is a million a lot?	212

JUNE

Don't trust Alex.	217
Life in our village.	220

Sing a song of sixpence, a pocket full of rye. Four and twenty blackbirds baked in a pie.	222
What Greek creature bit me?	225
Sometimes the Greek language can be really confusing.	227
Tomatoes only taste good in Greece.	230

JULY

Creating memories of Greece.	235
Funny Greek car hire.	239
Are you a thinker?	244
Are all Greek women so fit?	248
The art of canoeing in Greece	250
The philosophy of Alex.	253
I caught Covid	256
Just to get the blood pumping.	258

AUGUST

Decorating the garden.	265
Adjusting your bits	267
Catching pneumonia...in August.	270
Alex with a chainsaw.	274
Tasteful Greek garden design.	276
Alex strikes again.	278

Greek ferry trip. (Part 1) 280
Greek ferry trip. (Part 2) 284
Driving through France. 288
Meet Bella, our Anglo-Greek dog. 289
A fine dining experience. What, no souvlaki? 293
At last! Home in our village. 296
Relax. You're in Greece. 298
Cool and sexy. 300

SEPTEMBER

My birthday. 305
Horses bite! 307
Don't mess with the customs officer. 310
How to upset a Greek tortoise. 314
Secrets revealed. 317
Greece is a lovely country, but why is everything uphill? 320
Philosophy for all. Like it or not. 323
Boats hate me 325

OCTOBER

Greek wine. It's an acquired taste. 331
Peace and quiet in our village. 334

How to become more Greek: Lesson 1.	336
Alex shines in Chicago.	339
How to become more Greek: Lesson 2.	341
How to become more Greek: Lesson 3.	345
Informality at the airport.	347
Happy memories of summer.	351
Misunderstanding in Greece.	354

NOVEMBER

Irish coffee made difficult.	359
Autumn in our village.	362
A simple life in my Greek village.	365
As it's Sunday, I thought I would change the tone a little.	368
Greece is not perfect.	371
"Every heart sings a song, incomplete, until another heart whispers back." – Plato	375
Greek fishing adventures.	377
Living on a Greek island.	380

DECEMBER

The gang's all here.	385
The little house on the hill.	387

My Greek wife is trying to kill me.	390
Our little village, Glyfada.	393
Good afternoon Greece.	397
Life in a Greek island village.	402
The Greek monkey who changed history.	404
I don't want a swimming pool.	407
Our village is hibernating for the winter.	410
Lunch on the hoof.	414
Today we economised.	417
Greece always wins in the end.	420
Greek music is the best.	424
Dancing in our village.	427
The Kallikantzari.	430
Christmas Day.	434
Exploding pomegranates and cake on the ceiling.	437
A Note from the Author	440
About the Author	442
Contacts and Links	444
More Ant Press Books	446

A brief introduction.

Philosophy in Greece is not dead. It's alive and well through the musings of writer and thinker, Peter Barber. Peter is the author of the bestselling "Parthenon" series and his home is mostly on a sleepy Greek island.

Peter spends his time unsuccessfully trying to learn the Greek language, then resorting to the tried and tested way of communication every Englishman uses: speaking loudly in a mixture of broken Greek and English while pointing and waving his arms in the air. After years of patient practice, he has become the worst fisherman on his island, a sailor with no sense of direction, a wrecker of boats, and a keen gardener who has no idea how to differentiate weeds from useful plants. He is also an accomplished winemaker who rapidly became proficient at producing the best vinegar in the village, an unwitting entertainer of the village, and a collector of local wildlife. He is proud to share his view of life while drafting his books.

With these musings, it is clear where his sense of humour comes from. Peter is married to Alex, a fiery, loving and unpredictable Greek wife. It is a marriage made in comedy heaven.

Join Peter for a year of philosophy from Greece. Read on and smile.

January
IN OUR GREEK VILLAGE

Greece is changing, but not my village.

I love writing these musings about my Greek village. I feel like an athlete warming up for the main event.

Every day, I sit at my keyboard, ready for another day of book writing. But as I stare at the blank screen, waiting for inspiration, my mind wanders to Maria, who yesterday had a squabble with her brother, who lives next door to her house, about the water coming through his wall and soaking her carpet.

I think of the complaints from the village fisherman sitting in the *kafenio*, that the wind changed yesterday, and the fish weren't biting.

Vassilis was upset because his tractor had broken down, and Costas, the local tractor mender, was out of town, so he couldn't plough his field today.

Problems are a little different here. We don't seem to take any notice of the gossip in the outside world. We have enough of our own here. Someone in the British royal family broke their necklace, but we are not interested in that. We don't care about which celebrity is launching their new brand of perfume, or which Hollywood actor is divorcing his tenth wife.

In our village, we have a different outlook on life. We don't worry about the outside world. The important thing here is living our own lives. There is no need for a newspaper to catch up on the news. A visit to the *kafenio* is all you need to catch up on the important stuff.

But what this does is to promote an incredible community spirit. Talking brings people together. Not only do you receive the relevant news of the village, but because everyone is talking to everyone, we build friendships and bind the community.

But will this last?

A few days ago, I was sitting outside a coffee bar in Glyfada, near Athens. It was strangely quiet. The next table was full of several old men who would usually be speaking loudly over each other, arguing about their own political parties, and which football team is superior. But this time, each of them was staring into their own iPhones, stabbing the screen with their fingers. No talking, just absolute silence.

For me, this is scary. Is this the end of life as we know it? Are communities going to collapse because of a little black box? Luckily, in our village, we still talk. That's why I love living here.

Good morning and Happy New Year.
LET'S KICK OFF 2022 WITH A RANT.

Our first job after landing in Athens was to pass by the electrical superstore. Our cooker blew up on the last day we were here, so we needed a replacement. A security guard stopped us as we entered the store and demanded our Covid papers and passport, which he scanned before allowing us into the shop. Inside, all the employees were wearing double masks. So, we struggled a little to understand the muffled exchange but managed in the end.

Cooker ordered, we drove to the seaside to visit our favourite fish restaurant for our traditional arrival meal. As we entered, three double mask-wearing waiters blocked our way and asked for our Covid papers. Again, they were scanned before we could enter.

The next day, I wandered through Glyfada and sat for a coffee under a tree on the pavement outside a coffee house. The young waitress came over to my table with a scanner and asked for my Covid papers and passport.

Far from being upset by this intrusion, it impressed me. Greece is doing everything she can to minimise the spread of Covid and with the full agreement of the people.

In the UK, people are catching Covid in record numbers. Wearing a mask and showing "Covid Passports" are seen as an infringement of civil rights. This is backed up and actively encouraged by the elements of the British government. The right-wing press has always been critical of showing proof of vaccination and has condemned the use of masks, calling them "face nappies". Considering the amount of crap they talk, they all need a double nappy on both ends. If these suicidal individuals want to catch Covid, that's fine, but don't give it to me.

So who has it right??

Greece never ceases to impress me. The people know common sense when they see it, and all pull together as one to pass this difficult period in history with a smile behind their double masks.

Bravo Greece.

How Greek have I become?

We needed to prepare for the midnight celebration, Greek style.

First, we decided to redecorate the kitchen. We achieved this with nothing more than a food mixer used to make the *vasilopita* (traditional Greek New Year cake). By the time I had finished, four sweet-smelling cakes sat proudly as cake mix dripped from the ceiling, ran down kitchen cabinets and smeared over the windows.

But the cakes looked good. Every Greek family has its *vasilopita,* concealing a lucky coin.

A large onion wrapped in a Santa cloak with green leaves poking out of the top is hung above the door. This was traditionally used by

Greeks in ancient times to worship Pan, god of the wilds and of nature. This onion, even when uprooted, will continue to grow layers and blossom; it's said to have magical powers and is the symbol of rebirth. At midnight it's taken down and in the morning the children of the family are hit on the head with it to wake them up so that they can attend the church service for Saint Vassilis.

As midnight approached, the feast was arranged on the table and glasses charged to give thanks to the old year, and celebrate the new. A few moments before the magic hour, we ran around the house switching on all the lights, and turned on all the taps to allow water to run. All windows are opened to let out the *kallikantzaroi*: evil spirits, or mischievous Christmas goblins.

Then, on the stroke of midnight, my wife and I ran around the house frightening the dogs and neighbours, banging saucepans with wooden spoons to make as much noise as possible.

We then lifted our glasses and spat on each other (*Tou Tou To*) to ward off the bad eye and made a toast to the new year.

Then comes the *kalo podariko* (first footing) and pomegranate smashing. The lights are turned off. We step outside into the street and turn around to re-enter our house. It's important to enter with your right foot first. Then the pomegranate is thrown onto the floor, where it smashes, spilling out its seeds to symbolise abundance and leaving a lasting impression of red juice stains to remind you of the occasion. The more seeds, the better! This helps ensure luck, health, happiness and prosperity for the coming year.

After midnight, the *vasilopita* is sliced. We scored a cross over the surface, and the first slice is for Jesus Christ, the second for the Virgin Mary, the third for Saint Vassilis, the fourth for the house and then a slice for each member of the family, starting with the oldest. Whoever finds the lucky coin has good luck and good fortune for the rest of the year. Then the Christmas presents are opened.

Since I was lucky enough to marry a Greek wife many years ago, our cultures have merged. We have both taken the best of each other's.

Happy New Year to everyone.

It's snowing. Yes, in Greece.

We were driving up the mountain from Arachova towards the ski resort. The town was damp and drizzly, but although there were people wandering around wearing bobble hats, puffer jackets and skis over their shoulders, there was no snow to be seen.

Perhaps it has melted, I thought as we drove higher through the clouds.

Slowly, the snow appeared, first in small white streaks on the earth banks, then quickly the fields were turning white as we drove higher. Soon, we found ourselves driving in the furrows left by other vehicles. It was beautiful.

"Stop!" A policeman was standing in the

road with his hands raised. "Where are your *alysides chioniou*?"

I had never heard of snow chains until I arrived in Greece. On rare snow days in England, I just slowly followed cars in front of me, drove through the brown slush and took it easy. There was always a little sliding around, but snow was rare where I lived. I certainly never saw snow chains on any vehicles.

We were not allowed to go any further without them and were sent back down the mountain to buy some.

With a bag holding the *alysides chioniou*, we drove back up the mountain. As the road became white, I stopped to fit them onto the wheels. I opened the bag and pulled out a long-tangled mess of silver-linked metal with hooks and bits of red plastic attached.

I was expecting to open the bag, pop them on the wheels, and happily continue our drive up the mountain. Here, lying on the snow before me, was a MENSA puzzle. I looked at the picture on the bag. It just showed a wheel covered neatly by a chain, which had no resemblance to what was lying on the snow in front of me. It was snowing hard now, and I was getting colder.

I got one chain and wrapped it around the

rear wheel. It fell off onto the axle and got stuck there. I tried to pull it off, and it became more jammed. After laying myself down in the snow with my head under the car, I freed it. This went on for an hour. Me trying to fit the chains and the chains falling off and getting stuck.

I finally snapped the last connection into place with blue, numb fingers and stood back to admire my work. It didn't look good. Most of the chain was strapped to the wheel, but I had a lot of bits not connected to anything, just hanging limp. But that couldn't be helped. I had the other wheel to do.

I had developed hypothermia by the time I finished and got back into the car with Alex to warm up.

We were off up the mountain. I put my foot on the gas. The car didn't move. I pressed harder as the wheels spun in the snow.

How was I to know it was a front-wheel drive car? Nobody had told me that when I hired it.

Hooker or Hookah?

Yesterday we arrived in Arachova. We are renting a charming villa up in the mountains, which is part of a hotel complex. In our room we found a flyer offering a hookah which could be delivered by the hotel. I gave up smoking several years ago, but as this is not tobacco, I was tempted to order one.

I haven't tried it yet as I am struggling with how to call room service and ask them to bring me one. If they got that order wrong, I have a feeling my wife might bury me in the snowdrift outside.

We older people should know our limits.

I dream of playing the grand piano in packed concert halls in front of appreciative audiences. But I can't play the piano and am probably tone-deaf.

I could become a chess master and enter high-prestige tournaments worldwide, but I am held back by the small detail that I'm no good at chess. Alex beats me to death every time we play.

So I decided to try something even harder and learn to speak Greek fluently.

For over twenty years, Alex has been teaching me the wrong Greek. I stopped taking lessons from her a long time ago after getting myself into trouble in bread shops, petrol stations and pharmacies, asking for the most embarrassing things, while I believed I was just using the Greek language to ask for simple things like bread, petrol and aspirin. But, unknown to me at the time I was asking for other stuff – but I did entertain them.

I know all the swear words and how to use them for the best effect. I was competent in restaurants ordering food and could have simple conversations using broken Greek and hand signals. (Not the ones Alex taught me though!)

So, I asked a real teacher to help me.

Wow. The Greek language is really hard. The last two weeks have been a blur. I have learned that most Greek things have a gender. Beer is female, coffee is male, fruit is neutral, but the juice of the fruit is female. Work that out. Not only do I have to remember the sex of what I want, but the prefix to the sentence also changes, together with the words in the sentence. Asking for directions presents its own challenge. Streets have all three genders. Not only do you need to know where you're going, but you also need to know what sex it is. That's why you see so many lost tourists walking in circles waving maps in the air.

So, with three lessons a week, so far, I have only learned one thing. I'm stupid with languages. But with determination, I will get there in the end.

I have no sympathy from my dear Greek wife.

"Alex, Greek is a really hard language," I complained.

"Not for Greeks," she replied and wandered off.

Meanwhile, my lovely, patient Greek teacher peers at me through the screen with a reassuring smile before ending the lesson and going to have a lie down to recover.

Once I have mastered fluent Greek, I thought I would try something less challenging like rocket science or brain surgery.

Have a lovely weekend. I will be sleeping all weekend. I need the energy for next week's lessons. But only if my Greek teacher has recovered.

The eye.

The evil eye (*to kako mati*) is the most feared affliction in Greece. You can catch it if others are jealous of you, if you receive excessive compliments, or even by just being told your hair looks good today.

If I wear a new shirt and it looks nice, Alex will spit on me three times and using three fingers make a sign of the cross to ward off the eye. If you feel poorly or tired, it's unlikely to be an illness; rather it's a sign that you have caught the eye.

The only way to get rid of this affliction is by having a special prayer offered on your behalf by an older woman. The prayer for the eye is a closely guarded secret; it is told to a daughter by her mother.

One day a while back, I'd woken up late after a night out with some friends at a local bar in Glyfada. We'd been celebrating our win at a cricket match; the British expats having beaten the British Embassy team. We'd spent most of the evening trying to explain the rules of cricket to some Greeks, who eventually gave up trying to understand and suggested getting drunk instead. Not being a big drinker, I was now suffering the effects of having overdone it.

As I lifted my thumping head from the pillow, I was reminded of the enormous quantities of *ouzo* I'd consumed. I staggered into the bathroom and looked in the mirror. My face was pale, I had bags under my eyes, and my teeth felt hairy. I went downstairs to the terrace to get some coffee and an aspirin. Alex's mother, Debbie, was at the table peeling potatoes. When she glanced up at me, a sympathetic expression spread across her face.

"Oh, you poor thing, you have the eye," she said.

Not wishing to admit to my drunkenness of the night before, this seemed like a good excuse, so I readily agreed with her diagnosis. She went inside and returned with a mug of coffee.

"Just sit there, drink your coffee, and I will deal with the eye."

She then sat down beside me and prayed. After a few moments, tears rolled down her face and dripped onto the plastic tablecloth. For some reason, I started to yawn. Seconds later, she finished, and I felt better. I was well into my second cup of coffee when Alex came home, wheeling her trolley bag. She had been to the local market for some fruit and vegetables. She appraised my face and immediately ratted on me.

"I expected you to look a lot worse after coming home so drunk last night," she scolded.

Debbie leapt to my defence. "He may have had a little to drink," she said, "but he must have got the eye at that bar. I did the prayer, and he had a lot of eye, but he's fine now."

Alex's face softened as she sat down beside me. I could see I might yet get away with this.

"When Mum did the eye for you, did you yawn?" she asked.

"Yes, many times."

She was convinced. This had nothing to do with the vast quantity of booze consumed; I had been afflicted by the evil eye. She took my hand and, with a look of concern, assured me that I would start feeling better now that Debbie had done the prayer.

Strangely, I did feel better.

In Greece, cats chase dogs.

These charming little characters make their living by being lovely and cute. All *tavernas* have their resident moggies who charm you into releasing tasty titbits from your plate by rubbing against your legs and purring loudly.

I arrived at my village house recently after a period away. Within one day of arrival, there were four purring felines outside my door, waiting for their bowl of "Kitty Cat". The next day a few more had arrived. By the end of the week there were fourteen.

All was peaceful until a local dog unwisely wandered past my driveway. All fourteen cats suddenly transformed into blurry balls of fur and claws as they set off in pursuit of the unfortunate hound. As the dog ran, some cats, satisfied that they had seen off the stranger, gave up the chase and left, with their tails proudly held in the air. Others continued the chase. In the distance, I watched as two of the cats caught the dog and were both glued to its back, hanging on with claws extended. Another had got in front and was launching a head-on attack.

I wondered why all the dogs in our village avoided cats and why the dogs all had scars on their faces. I soon worked out these cuddly pussy cats were actually miniature hybrid leopards pretending to be cats. Mystery solved.

Some things in Greece are different. I love living here.

Adventure with Avis

We spend our time between the UK, Athens, and our Greek village, Pefki, on the island of Evia. Because I left our car standing at our village home over the winter months, a family of mice moved into the engine and feasted on the cables.

So this time, we had to hire a car until we could evict the local wildlife and arrange repairs.

We arrived at Athens airport, picked up our hire car and left for the drive to the village. I'm not a speed freak and drive at old-man speed, avoiding the temptation to race. So, I didn't bother with the excess insurance cover.

A few days later, we drove to the supermarket to get some supplies. As I opened the car boot to pack the carrier bags, I noticed a big dent in the rear bumper. Someone had hit me and driven away without leaving a note. This was inconvenient. It would cost me a fortune when the hire company saw it.

I had an idea. I would take it to a repair company, get it fixed cheaper than the hire company would charge, and they would be none the wiser. A good plan, or so I thought. The repair shop removed the bumper, rubbed out the scratches and repainted the bodywork. A couple of hundred euros later, the repair looked good, with no evidence of the sneaky fix.

Back at the airport, I crossed my fingers as the Avis representative holding a clipboard walked around the car for his inspection. He checked the fuel, recorded the mileage, and began the external checks. Suddenly, he stopped at the area of the repair. Looked at his clipboard. Looked at the bumper. He seemed confused.

"Is everything OK?" I asked.

"No, we have a problem," he replied.

Damn it. I'd been busted.

He turned his back and went into the office, and emerged with his supervisor. Both stood there, running their hands over the repaired area, looking perplexed.

Eventually, one of them spoke in broken English.

"What happened here? When you took the car, it had a dent in the bumper. Now it's gone."

I didn't bother to check the condition report when I rented the car, which, unknown to me, was already damaged.

"Perhaps it healed itself," I replied unconvincingly, and not wishing to look as stupid as I felt, hurried away to catch our flight.

What a plonker.

How Greece has changed!

My wife grew up in Glyfada, a seaside suburb of Athens. Back then, it was a village. Some roads were just compacted earth with no tarmac. They dotted the houses along these small streets, each with a small garden. Some had chickens scratching around, others fruit trees, or bougainvillaea and jasmine climbing over the white walls. Everyone in the street knew each other. Conversations were had over garden walls, or shouted across the dusty road. No one made an appointment to visit. They just turned up. It was one enormous family.

But change was coming.

Gradually, the villagers were tempted with the promise of wealth and allowed their family homes to be replaced with towering apartment blocks. Some villagers moved away with their new-found wealth. Others stayed and moved into their shiny new apartments and closed the door.

Within a few short years, Glyfada became a fashionable resort with high land prices, sophisticated bars and restaurants. But the village died. There were no more conversations over garden walls, no more wandering into each other's homes for a coffee. We had become distant from each other.

Life in the village is different. Thankfully, the villages and island itself still keep much of their character.

I decided to bake bread. I had a nice wood-fired oven that had only been used for pizza, but I wanted to try it for authentic Greek bread. Standing in my kitchen with flour up to my elbows, I was kneading dough. A finger came out of nowhere and poked at the mixture.

"Too dry," came a voice from behind me.

One of my neighbours had wandered in through the open back door, saw I was making bread and offered her advice. I thanked her and went to the sink for a little water to add to the mix. I turned back to my dough.

But she had taken over. She wasn't happy

with the way I was doing it, so she decided to do it for me. I left her to it and wandered into the garden. Then I heard the sound of sawing. Up a tree was another one of my neighbours. He had seen that a tree needed pruning, so brought his ladder and did it for me.

Living in this village, you are never alone. The village mayor will arrive on his moped for a coffee and a chat. The locals always pop in for a chat when passing. Our local farmer arrives to tell me how many trees I should plant. Even the shepherd will bring his goats for a visit. No one uses the front door or ever knocks. They just arrive and wander around the back and sit with us.

The time came to cook the bread. The oven was lit, and the loaf was rising nicely. My neighbour came over, looked at the beautifully risen loaf, pressed it down flat with both hands and put it into the oven. She preferred flat bread, and who was I to argue?

This is the old way, and it's beautiful. I love living here.

Ok. I agree. It's Greek.

Alex, my Greek wife, is a patriot and fiercely defends her cultural heritage. I was sitting at my keyboard writing when Alex looked over my shoulder at the screen.

"Did you know you're writing Greek?" she said.

"No, I'm writing in English." I replied, "Look." I pointed at the words on the screen and read a section.

"Yes, but the words you are writing have come from the Greek language."

"No, they haven't. This is the language of Shakespeare, Samuel Pepys and Francis Bacon. This is English."

"No, it's not. It's Greek," she persisted.

I stopped typing to listen to this new revelation.

She often reminds me that Greeks were writing novels while my ancestors still lived in trees. Poetry was being recited in the Athens marketplace before we discovered rocks. But this was a new one.

She went on.

"Look, your book is mostly comedy. This is a Greek word. Κωμωδία (*komodeea*). You have just finished an episode, Επεισόδιο (*episodeio*), you keep drifting off into fantasy with your writing until I tell you to stop, Φαντασία (*fantasia*). Even words like helicopter, Ελικόπτερο (*elikoptero*) are Greek, you idiot: Ιδιώτης (*idiotes*)."

I was just imagining the ancient philosophers buzzing around in helicopters, but I didn't really want to point this out to Alex. She was obviously bored and needed to pick a fight.

"OK, OK, I agree. Just leave me to write," I pleaded.

"Yes, and OK is Greek too," she claimed. "'*Ola Kala*' (όλα καλά), meaning 'all good'."

Well, this was interesting. I thought I had been writing a book in English. But now realise that not only am I writing about life in our Greek village, but I'm also writing it in Greek. I'm cleverer than I thought.

Alex in trouble (again).

We went to a nearby village for lunch near the harbour. There is a row of fish *tavernas* and cafes in a line, all overlooking beautiful scenery with a superb view of the boats. It's a charming village and well known for the fresh fish unloaded from the tiny boats straight to the kitchens of the *tavernas*, so it is always fresh.

There was the usual assortment of local wildlife. Seagulls perched on the top of lampposts and canopies, waiting for an opportunity to swoop down and snaffle an unguarded piece of fish. The sparrows fussed around the table, stealing pieces of bread and the odd chip before flying away with their treasure. The local cats were performing their usual antics of charming the tourists with loud purrs to gain favour, and some of their meals. But today, the stray dogs were out of luck. They knew the cats would be favoured, so they just snoozed in the shade, waiting their turn.

We had finished our meal, so I took some bread and walked the few steps to the harbour wall to feed the grey mullet. Alex had shooed the cats away and had made friends with a stray dog and was feeding him scraps.

As we left, I saw her scraping our plates onto the floor in front of her new friend before joining me for the walk to the car.

A few days later, we returned to the same *taverna*, took our usual table, and sat looking at the view while waiting to order.

The owner came out, stopped, and looked at Alex.

"So, it's you, is it?"

"Hello," Alex sweetly replied.

It impressed me that the *taverna* owners always remembered us. We usually left a good tip and made new friends often. But today, they remembered us for a different reason.

"Madam, last time you were here, you put your food on the floor. The dog didn't eat it, and I didn't see it until I slipped in the mess, nearly fell in the sea, got pasta sauce in my bottom crack, then tramped it all back into the restaurant. We had to clean the outside area and mop the entire kitchen. I would be grateful if you didn't do that again."

Alex was completely unfazed by this telling-off and just looked at him over the top of her menu.

"OK," she replied. "What's good today? Got any sardines?"

"Fried or grilled?" he asked.

Mosquitos are stupid.

Spending most of my summers scratching lumpy bites, smothering myself in citronella and always smelling of lemons is my personal war against these ferocious little predators.

I have tried all the local cures, such as rubbing basil onto my arms and legs, only to find the mosquitos prefer green skin. The villagers' suggestion of drinking a bottle of *ouzo* didn't work either. The mosquitos just brought friends and had a party with me as their buffet.

But help is at hand. A recent scientific study revealed that mosquitos are stupid. Researchers have found that these blood-sucking predators are attracted to *pantzári* (beetroot) because it is the same colour as their favourite food, blood, but when they stick their sharp little noses into the vegetable, they also receive a dose of the natural insecticide contained within the skin and swiftly die. Scientists are now looking at this as a malaria control measure.

I am looking at this as a way of not being eaten alive on warm evenings. So, I need to plan carefully. First, I need to buy all the *pantzári* on the island. A truckload should do it. Then invest in a few industrial cookers to boil them, being careful not to damage the precious skin. Then hang them in bunches all around my garden and above my bed and wait.

The only downside to this idea is: I hate beetroot.

Will I be attracting every mosquito on the island to visit my house?

I will probably combine the red juice pooling on the floor with actual blood when my wife finds out the house has turned red, and the lawn has changed colour.

But in the name of advancing scientific discovery, I will take that chance for the good of mankind and all puffy tourists who forgot to pack the repellent.

Look into her eyes.

The UK government has instructed Brits to ditch face masks. Greece asks you to wear two!!

In Greece, in all indoor and outdoor public spaces, in areas such as supermarkets and pharmacies, and on public transport, you will be required to wear either double masks (at least one of which should be surgical) or an N95/FFP2 mask. What do the Brits know that the Greeks don't?

My theory is that the British government are much more concerned about killing its economy, rather than killing its population. Seeing that the already damaged economy would plummet still further if masks were worn. As a mask would cover most of your face and there would no longer be any need to make an effort.

Lipstick and cosmetic suppliers are already suffering. Teeth whitening kits are no longer required. Cosmetic surgeons found that Botox and lip fillers have suffered their biggest ever decline and people that offer nose and lip piercing are seeing the bottom fall out of their business as the wearers of exotic nose rings will no longer be able to frighten children, so there is no point, and the lip studs snag the masks.

I personally think people look good in masks. We now have to look into each other's eyes as the only way to become more aware of emotions. It's no good waiting for a frown or a smile.

My Greek wife has always been good at melting glass with a stare. Now more of us men must develop this talent of reading eyes and knowing when to run away. Don't worry, natural selection will take care of this. The ones that fail to recognise the danger signals just won't survive in the future.

Writing about Greece.

I write about Greece. It doesn't take too much imagination. I just look out of the window and see the beauty of my subject spread around me.

The bright Greek sunshine in an unreal blue sky, orange and lemon trees swaying gently in the cool breeze, the sound of the crickets, the perfume of mountain herbs invading my senses and the distant tinkle of bells tied to the collars of local goats grazing happily on the hills.

This is all lovely. However, I'm much more interested in the antics of my neighbour, Yiannis, who sat on the wrong side of the branch while pruning his tree with a chainsaw yesterday. He survived the fall, but the chainsaw didn't. Or Costas, the local fisherman who found the best spot ever with an unlimited number of fish. He had stumbled upon a nearby fish farm and thought it was his birthday.

I was sitting in the cafe listening to one group of locals discussing a nearby village where a wind farm was erected the previous year:

"I don't know why they want to make more wind," one old gentleman said. "You can understand why they want this big fan on the hill in summer because it gets hot. But in wintertime, it's cold enough, so they should turn it off."

Lots of writers can describe the magnificent beauty of Greece much better than I do. With my books, I just love to make people smile. I focus my words on life in Greece and my adapting to the culture after marrying my feisty Greek wife.

It's been a wonderful journey, sometimes sad, often frustrating, but mostly hilarious. In these dark days of conflict in our world, let's take a break from the news, enter our own protected space, and keep smiling together. I hope my humorous musings about this beautiful country will help.

February

IN OUR GREEK VILLAGE

Writing about Greece can be really dangerous.

But having a Greek wife who is passionate about her country and heritage, it's doubly so.

In the morning, I sit at my desk, ready to create the next epic saga of Greek life.

Crash helmet on. Check.

Fireproof underwear. Check.

Bulletproof vest. Check.

I begin to write. I feel a hot breath on the back of my neck. Alex is reading my words. I start to panic, my hands sweat. Feeling like Indiana Jones in the Temple of Doom, I pick my way over the keyboard, being careful not to tread on the paving stones, which are likely to collapse, sending me plummeting into the abyss. I head towards the holy grail, trying to avoid the traps designed to decapitate the unwary. I continue past the trigger that releases the giant rocks which will crush the life from my body. I finally sneak around the deadly instruments of death and see my treasure ahead. Then, the terrifying phrase is uttered.

"You can't write that!"

Alex has seen my script and is getting annoyed.

"How dare you write that? It's not true."

"But I have checked the documents. Even Wikipedia agrees." I showed her the entry.

"Baklava, a dessert popular throughout the Middle East, originated in Turkey in the eleventh century and is thought to have been invented by nomadic Turks. The Turkish word *yuvgha*, which translates as 'pleated or folded bread', is thought to be a crucial piece of evidence for the origin of baklava."

"Propaganda," she replied. "My mother would never have cooked a Turkish dish. The neighbours would never forgive her."

"But you eat kebabs," I ventured.

"We have never eaten kebabs in Greece. We don't need to. We have *souvlaki*, which is much better."

That told me.

Sore heads and Spam on the side

Alex and I are not talking. Every sound is deafening. Our heads are thumping, and I am seeing double. My mouth feels like I have been eating sand, and my teeth have gone hairy. We are currently sitting in our garden whispering a pledge. We will never drink wine again!

Yesterday we had an interesting lunch at the local *taverna*. As usual, our eyes were bigger than our bellies.

"You are not leaving until you have eaten my food," Pavlos scolded.

"But we are stuffed," I protested. "We can't possibly eat all that. It's not our fault this time."

Pavlos is a loud, rough, strict man who

takes pride in his cooking. He often gets upset with us because we usually order too much and take it home for the cats. So, this time we allowed him to recommend the food and order for us. First, a kilo of wine arrived with three glasses. Dish after dish was served. barbecue lamb cutlets, grilled liver, a huge Greek salad, fried potatoes, tzatziki, and cheese dip. Then, a surprising plate of Spam.

We tried to plough through the dishes but were beaten by the quantity, and I'm not very keen on Spam.

We continued eating and watched as the last clients paid their bill, leaving us alone with the owner. He was determined to keep us prisoner until we had presented clean plates. It was now time for his lunch, and he emerged from the kitchen carrying yet another enormous plate of food and a jug of wine. He pulled out a chair and sat at our table, poured wine into our glasses and filled his to the brim. He had joined us so he could keep a watchful eye in case we escaped.

We chatted while pushing our food around our plates, looking for one of the *taverna* cats to save us. But they were full and sleeping under the tree in the shade, so no help there.

The conversation flowed with the wine.

Before we even realised, two jugs were empty, and he yelled into the kitchen for more. Another two appeared, followed by several more. I soon lost count as the world slowly became a better place. The cold wine created a warm embrace as the world began to spin, and my face went numb. I looked at Alex. She had gone cross-eyed and was looking abnormally pink. She rarely drinks, so was suffering. Without noticing, we were sipping the wine and then taking a bite of food until the meal ended. We even ate the Spam.

Every time the wine jug emptied, someone instantly replenished it. We heard about his upbringing, and his love of cooking and life in the village. Family secrets were shared. We realised he was a sensitive soul, and we had broken through his rough shell to reveal an incredible kindness. And over the food and vast quantities of homemade wine, we made yet another lifelong friend.

I hear he had a delivery of some excellent calamari this morning, so perhaps we will go again today. No more wine though ... Oh, OK, but only if he insists – it would be rude to refuse.

"The energy of the mind is the essence of life" – *Aristotle*

I'm now at risk of the affliction that has affected every older person in history. I have complained about the younger people of today. I don't remember when it began, I simply started using the phrases "In my day" and "When I was young".

Oh my God, I am getting old.

I noticed when I went to my opticians in Athens. As I entered the shop, a spotty teenage chap was behind the reception desk, tapping away at his phone. Without looking up, he muttered, "Yes?" I didn't answer. I waited for him to give me his full attention. After a few moments, it was clear his social media was far more important than me.

I said in a loud voice, "Are you with me, or shall I come back later?" This shocked him out of his virtual world and into mine. He put his phone in his pocket and directed me to the optician, who tested my eyes.

I needed a slight prescription change. So, I went back to the spotty youth, who tapped at his computer, ordered the new glasses and asked me to come back the following week. A few days later, I returned to collect them. I put them on and saw double. "These don't work," I told him. Assuming I was senile, he spoke slowly so I could understand.

"It's. A. Change. Of. Prescription. You. Have. To. Get. Used. To. Them."

I looked back at the spotty assistant, who now had a twin. I closed one eye and his brother disappeared, and I replied equally slowly.

"But. I. Can't. Bloody. See!"

He gave me an exasperated look, picked up the phone and called the optician, who came over. He checked my glasses and inspected the computer screen.

"Oh, I see the problem. There has been a typo. Instead of your correct prescription of

+1.75, someone has changed it to -1.75. That's why you can't see." He cast an accusing look at the sheepish assistant.

In Greek villages, youngsters seem to be more switched on. In most of the islands and rural parts, they work with their families and learn the old ways, devoid of invasive modern technology. But in the cities, things seem to be dumbing down.

Our washing machine in Glyfada blew up, so we needed a new one. We selected the model, paid for it, and arranged for delivery, removal of the old one, and connection. The next day, two young men arrived with the new appliance. They pulled out the old machine, stood back and scratched their heads.

"This is impossible," one said. "Look, there's a water pipe. We can't connect this; you will need a specialist."

"But it's a washing machine, it runs on water. Surely you know this?" I said.

They were still unwilling to tackle the difficult task of unscrewing two pipes and reconnecting them. So I turned the water off at the tap, unscrewed the pipe and asked them to take the old one away. By the time they had loaded it into their van, I had connected the new one myself and was halfway through the first wash load.

I think I have worked it out. In today's world of instant gratification, we no longer need to think for ourselves. The seeking of knowledge requires curiosity. A quick Google search will tell you what you want to know, but you have missed the journey of gaining knowledge along the way. "In my day", we went to a library to look something up. Before finding our goal we learned other wonderful stuff in the meantime. This is curiosity and the reason we learn.

I think the world is doomed to slip into a fog of stupidity. AI, social media, fake news and conspiracy theories rule our lives.

But in the land of the blind, the one-eyed man is king. Which is a good thing, because my new spectacles aren't ready yet.

Am I sad or proud?

Perhaps a little of both.

Yesterday, we visited the small seaside village of Castella, a suburb of Piraeus. It's the village where Alex's mother, Debbie, was born and raised. As a young girl, she would swim happily among the old wooden fishing boats. She would spend her days chatting with the fishermen, busy mending their nets, while her mother watched from the house on the hill as she cooked the family lunch.

When Alex and I were first married, we would take Debbie back to her village for lunch at one of the beautiful old fish *tavernas* which surrounded the harbour. We would step down from the road and take a seat on the edge of the water. Debbie would tell us stories about her family while pointing up at the hill, showing us where her friends lived. She would tell us of her sea captain father, and the joy she felt every time he returned from sea. She would fascinate us with stories of the war years and the suffering of the village, and happiness when peace returned to Greece.

From our seats in the traditional *taverna*, we could have stepped onto the old blue fishing boats. We would sit and enjoy the typical food of the village off blue wooden tables with plastic tablecloths and rickety chairs. We would throw scraps to the grey mullet and watch as the water boiled with thousands of fish, eager to get their piece of bread or shrimp shell.

Since Debbie passed away, we hadn't returned to this beautiful village, so we were unaware of the changes.

Yesterday, Alex had an idea.

"Let's go to Mum's village for lunch. We haven't been for ages," she said.

We drove into Castella to find our favourite *taverna*. Everything had changed. The old *tavernas* had been demolished and rebuilt away from the harbour wall. Where we used to sit was now a new pedestrian walkway separating the restaurants from the water. They all had smart new tables with starched cotton tablecloths. The waiters had uniforms. In place of the local food was a new menu advertising gourmet dishes, and in place of the red tin jugs of wine, we now had a wine list.

I felt as if I had left Greece and was now sitting at a sterile, upmarket restaurant on the French Riviera, with prices to match. Things must change. But why this village?

Yes, I am proud of Greece. But also a little sad.

My famous wife.

I'm busily putting the final touches to my new book. It's almost ready to send off to my editor. She will somehow convert my incoherent ramblings into something readable. Good luck with that.

I never get writers' block. With me, it's the other way. My butterfly mind is always so full of information, all jumbled up and buzzing around like the contents of Alex's handbag. I start writing about being banned from the local village *taverna* and end up discussing how to escape from a ravenous octopus. Then I think of a funny story that would make a nice Facebook post and write that instead.

I remember going with Alex to see the funny Greek Canadian Angelo Tsarouchas in

London. The audience was mostly Greeks living in England.

We arrived at the swish London venue and joined the queue. As we entered, the girl checking our tickets looked up.

"You're Alex," she smiled. "I've just been reading about you."

I was proud. My book was even more popular than I thought. It was selling well. But this was my first experience where someone had actually recognised us. Maybe we were becoming celebrities.

"Have you read about her in my book?" I asked.

I was thinking of bragging about my literary creation and was even going to offer to sign it for her. If she didn't have her copy to hand, I may have a spare copy in the car. It was only parked a mile away.

"No, what book?" she asked and turned back to Alex. "I've just been reading about you on Facebook. I saw your name on the list so I've saved you a seat right at the front."

She smiled in my direction and led us into the theatre. As we walked, people stopped, looked at Alex and smiled. Some said hello and others wanted to stand and chat. I felt like

Prince Phillip following the Queen a few paces behind.

"You're famous," I teased as we took our seats.

I went to the bar to buy our drinks and returned to a huddle of people around Alex. They were chatting and laughing as I took my seat when they left. They hadn't heard about the book either. But they were all Facebook enthusiasts. When Angelo came on stage, I expected him to wave at Alex, but the spotlight must have been in his eyes, and he missed the chance.

So, if you're looking for fame, don't write a book, marry a Greek.

Living in Greece. Know the rules.

Living with a fiery Greek wife is exciting. She is a little firework. When her fuse is lit, she fizzes slowly before the big bang, then goes out just as quickly. My wife has a wonderful openness which is refreshing for a foreigner, but you need to know the rules.

My wife sometimes asks what I am thinking. I usually answer: "Nothing," and I'm being honest.

This is not a concept understood by females. Males have the superpower of being able to shut down and stare into nothingness with absolutely no thoughts in their heads. Experience has taught me over the years that replying to this question in this way will only light the fire.

A lioness will always prowl around the savanna, looking for herds of prey, but does not attack at once. She will take her time hiding in the long grass, ears flattened against her head, while studying the herd, looking for a weak or vulnerable animal that wouldn't take too much catching and is unlikely to escape. Three hundred Spartan warriors almost defeated a Persian army of millions. Be warned, your wife has the same genes.

"You must be thinking of something," she is getting suspicious now.

Quickly my brain reactivates as I search for a thought that I might get away with. I try the standard one:

"I was just thinking how lovely you look today."

I realise she thinks that I have been caught out thinking about the waitress at the nearby *taverna* with the low-cut dress, or the bronzed girls sunbathing on the nearby beach. I'm now in trouble. Trying to defuse the situation, I reach out for other explanations.

"I had a hard day in the garden, worried about the moles under my lawn, and became concerned about the influence of global warming on squirrels." I'm getting desperate now.

I'm in a dark tunnel and the only light I can see is from the train coming. There is no way out.

Alex decides to pick away at my non-existent shell to get to the truth. Desperately I fumble for a reason that I had a blank look on my face, but any reason clutched at is not good enough and I must have a better one. After the standard grilling, and me promising to be good in the future, I usually return to staring into the distance but keeping a good excuse handy, in case I am interrogated again.

Men are simple creatures and generally honest. If asked if we have a problem, we usually answer truthfully. We have simple needs, are mostly oblivious to our environment, easy to keep and quite happy with the small pleasures in life.

But we need to know the rules.

"You don't like my food?"

Before I lived in Greece, I was trim and sprightly. I could look down and see my feet. My belly was flat. When I breathed in, I could feel my navel flapping on my backbone. If I showered, I would need to keep moving to get wet. Those were the days.

Debbie, my Greek mother-in-law, began my transition. She would cook huge amounts of scrumptious food, glistening stuffed tomatoes covered in golden olive oil straight from the wood oven. Giant *tiropitas* with rich creamy feta cheese and crispy golden filo pastry, Greek salads served in washing-up bowls with litres of oil, slabs of feta and oregano sprinkled over the top. A shoal of char-grilled red mullet followed this, then *calamari* fried to perfection with a few buckets of fried potatoes.

She would watch me with a concerned look as I ate.

"You are not hungry?" She would ask after my third loaded plate. "Eat something, you have eaten nothing," she would complain as she loaded up another plate and put it in front of me.

I would feel my belt tightening. Sweat would appear on my top lip as I tried to please her and eat all I was offered. But I could never win. Debbie would always walk away, sadly shaking her head, disappointed that I had eaten "nothing". Then she would return with a large cream cake with strawberries on top, a giant tray of *baklava* and a bucket of yoghurt covered with a kilo of honey to "help me digest."

By the time we arrived in our village home, I knew it was impossible to satisfy a Greek mother. I could have eaten the five offered plates, the entire *baklava*, consumed the table, legs and all. She would still walk away, sadly claiming I had eaten nothing.

My waistline had increased so much, I gave up wearing trousers in favour of elasticised joggers. This was because every time I wore trousers, they had shrunk a little more and the belt needed a new hole. I was finding my shower needed more water, and every time I got into the bath, I would flood the floor with the resulting tidal wave.

A Greek *taverna* would be different. I could just order what I wanted to eat. The problem was, another Greek mother ran and owned our local *taverna*. We would go for lunch. She would pile food onto the table without ordering. Lunch would turn into dinner as the Greek mother would sit watching me with a disappointed look as I munched my way through the offerings in a vain hope I wouldn't offend her.

But it always ended with the immortal phrase used by all Greek mothers: "Why you have eaten nothing? You don't like my food?"

It's Carnival time in Greece.

Today marks the last day before Lent in Greece. But we have one last chance to enjoy ourselves before the fasting starts. The best place to do this is in Patras, the main port for ferries to Italy, around two hundred kilometres north-west of Athens.

The city hosts one of the largest carnivals in the world, attracting almost half a million visitors every year during the season. The tradition of dressing up comes from the practice of women wearing masks to hide their identity. The Greeks took this a step further. Now everyone dresses up.

The first time Alex and I went to the carnival, Alex decided that she would dress as an Amazon warrior – highly appropriate, we agreed, given that, like Alex, the Amazons were famed for their aggression and brutality, with their primary concern in life being war.

She decreed that I would dress as Conan the Barbarian. As we had no chance of finding a hotel, we'd planned to sleep in the car. This had presented problems with getting into our costumes, but we managed.

Alex looked magnificent: slim and very sexy in her short leather skirt. After touching up her own makeup, she turned her attention to mine. She wanted to paint black flashes across my face to make me appear macho and fit the part of Conan the Barbarian. I sat patiently as she got to work but had no idea how I looked as the car mirror had recently fallen off my old Citroen and I hadn't had time to replace it.

I pulled on my platinum-blonde wig borrowed from Alex's beauty salon and we set off to join the festivities. The atmosphere in the crowded streets was lively. Thousands of people were dancing to loud, thumping music outside bars and filling the main squares, all wearing colourful costumes and having a great time.

As I stood watching the procession, I received a lot of attention from passing revellers. Some blew kisses in my direction; others grabbed my bottom and squeezed it before walking away with a smile on their faces.

I looked at Alex. She was giggling, her eyes wet with tears. She'd been watching and relishing the reactions I was getting. It took me a long time to cotton on, but finally, I realised why she'd taken such a long time painting my face earlier.

I rushed over to a nearby shop window to try and catch my reflection. It confirmed my suspicions. Staring back at me was not a warlike barbarian with black flashes, but a pantomime dame with dark blue eyeshadow, bright red lipstick and deep pink blusher, further enhanced by the blonde wig.

I had spent the afternoon walking around proudly, assuming I resembled Arnold Schwarzenegger, while I actually resembled one of my more eccentric aunties.

I'm not doing that again.

The sea is the way, they say.

Greece is a seafaring nation. Many of the men in our village have been to sea. Alex comes from a long line of sea captains. Greek wives historically became strong because their men were away from home for so long. They learned to live for many years without their loved ones. Missing became a way of life to most.

I was once asked to look at a piece of writing from an old Greek sailor which illustrates the hopes and dreams of one of these men. Thank you, Mina Mila. It touched my heart.

Chalo Yiannis.

The sea is the way, they say...

But I was seven years old, and I had no other way...

I was a poor farm boy, tired of working the rocky land all day for no reward.

So, one day I jumped onto the ship to become a "moutsos", a thankless job, the lowest of the low.

Years passed and my mistress, the sea, treated me well.

I worked hard and became a chief engineer.

Married, back on the island, my merry wife and two daughters waited, usually for years at a time.

1938: I was told we were sailing to London. A cargo of coal was waiting for us.

Who would have known a war was just around the corner?

I was trapped in London, looking for shelter away from the falling bombs.

I ran away, but luck brought me to Liverpool, where Mr Evans, the widower Englishman, gave me shelter and a job in his fish and chip shop.

But my mind would always drift back to my sacred paradise, and family left behind.

They had no way of knowing I was still alive and doing well.

And I had no way to know they were struggling to survive as the war spread back home, too.

Years passed slowly, but finally the war was over.

Mr Evans showed great generosity to my hard-working ethics.

I was now the owner of the shop, and on my way home to bring my family to England.

1947: I arrived home. I was walking through my village. Soon I would be at my house, I thought, never doubting my family was still waiting for me.

I saw a young woman at the spring. She smiled at me.

My oldest daughter should be at the same age, I thought ...

How could I know she was my daughter? I would see later in the house.

The sea is the way, they say ...

Now, I have two sons-in-law, both navy captains.

My daughters, as their mother before, trained to be captains of the land, rulers of their family. Will they live through the same lonely bitterness?

We, the sailors, brothers, cousins, neighbours, would find comfort at nights in dirty harbours. We talk and dream about the day we will be back home to smell the lemon blossom, the scented jasmine on warm summer evenings, the perfume of mountain herbs invading our senses, wafting down to the village, while watching the thunderstorms drifting above the mountains at night, cooling the air. We long to feel the warmth of the sun on our faces again.

Some of us made it...

Welcome to our island.

The new Durrells? Perhaps not.

I think I need to think again.
On Wednesday, I had a meeting in London with a film producer and production company who seem to be interested in turning my book into a TV series.

The meeting seemed to start well, but went downhill fast. Being a true story, and me insisting it remained true, seemed to unsettle them.

"We love the story, but need to change it a little for the screen."

"OK, how?" I asked.

"We think it needs some more conflict," one producer suggested.

"I think there is plenty of conflict. Alex tried to kill our builder frequently and me once. What more do you need? Extra blood, more details of him running along the road yelling for his mother pursued by an angry Alex waving a chunk of wood with a nail in it.? I can do that. After all, that happened."

They were angling towards the typical romantic comedy storyline.

Boy meets girl. Boy loses girl, Boy gets girl back. Happy ever after.

"Perhaps we can change Chapter 8. Maybe you have a fling with an exotic dancer and Alex leaves you. Then she forgives you in Chapter 10," they suggested.

"Listen. If I had a fling with an exotic dancer, Alex would have instantly killed me, and the exotic dancer, most of her family and pets, then buried us all under the real Parthenon. Then there would never have been a Chapter 10," I told them.

I hate these done-to-death storylines. They may sell movies, but it rarely works that way in real life. How many times have you watched a film where someone steps onto a road? There is a long-extended blare of a truck horn, then a crash as it crushed the poor victim under the wheels.

None of these clever film directors realises that if you had enough time for a thirty-second blast of the horn, you could have used your foot instead and stepped on the brake. Thus, no crash.

The meeting didn't go well. Maybe they will turn my book into a series. But perhaps only if I rewrite the script to turn myself into a philandering bad guy with a pencil-thin moustache and a reputation with the ladies. I don't think so.

So, I won't hold my breath. I can't think who would play the part of Alex, anyway. Being a cross between Zorba the Greek's more ferocious sister, a Spartan warrior with the face of an angel, and a nuclear missile with a Greek flag painted on the side. They would have to do a lot of auditions to fill that part.

Any suggestions?

March

IN OUR GREEK VILLAGE

The world's worst builders. (Part 1)

We had finished our house in the Greek village. Everything was working. Hot water, electricity – all fine. So, we turned our attention to the garden.

Building the house had cleared out our savings. We couldn't afford to hire a builder for our new patio. So, we did it ourselves. How hard can it be?

Early in the morning we went to the builders' merchant, found some natural stones that looked nice, and ordered a couple of jumbo bags of sand and a few bags of cement. Being a loving, considerate husband, I didn't want Alex to mix concrete by hand, so I took her to choose a cement mixer. She was delighted and chose a bright yellow one and a matching wheelbarrow.

The next day we were up early and started up the yellow mixer and set to work. First, we mixed a batch of cement, poured it onto the ground and set some of our stones on top. They sank below the surface, leaving only a few bubbles. The cement was too wet.

We made another mix with less water, poured it onto the ground and set some stones on that. The cement dried too quickly, leaving the stones sitting proudly on top of the base. This wouldn't have been too much of an issue if we had used standard thickness paving, but natural stones were of various thicknesses, some less than one inch, others over four inches thick.

"Okay," we thought. "Let's just lay the stones on top of the drying cement and sort it out later."

We agreed.

We went ahead and finished the patio. Although it looked rather like the surface of the moon, only with more craters, we were happy with our work. All we needed now was to cut the chair and table legs to make them level so we could sit and have a meal without the food sliding off.

MUSINGS FROM A GREEK VILLAGE

Next, we would build a roof over it.

The world's worst builders. (Part 2)

Our patio had dried. We spent the next week pouring cement into the craters, trying to level it out as much as possible. It still had a surface resembling a wavy day at the beach. We had to keep staring into the distance. If we focused for too long, we started to feel a little seasick, but we had our patio. It was certainly not perfect, but better than bare earth.

Next, we needed to put a roof over it. This was more in my comfort zone. I'm OK with a bit of carpentry and felt I could handle the framework. Alex and I went off to the builders' yard and ordered a truckload of timber and some roof tiles.

After we finished the timber frame, Alex's

job was to set the tiles. I was taking them up the ladder. Alex was jumping from joist to joist like a mountain goat, fitting the tiles in neat rows. Soon we had our new roof over our wavy patio. It looked fantastic. Then came testing time.

Alex went for a walk with the dogs while I put the garden hose on top of the tiles and switched it on full force. I climbed down the ladder to check underneath. It was raining: I moved the hose around, and everywhere I directed the water, it dripped through the tiles. Something was seriously wrong.

By the time Alex returned, I had worked out the problem. When we built the frame, there was not enough of a slope. So water was running backwards and coming through. Simple fix. I just needed to cut the support legs a little to give more of a fall. Problem solved.

Alex returned.

"We have a minor problem," I told her. "Water is coming through the tiles. But ..."

Before I had a chance to tell her the easy fix, her eyes darkened with rage. My Greek wife has the face of an angel, but the spirit of a warrior. She stomped off towards the car. She jumped into the driving seat; I leapt in beside her, trying to explain the easy cure.

But Alex was deaf to my explanation. As far as she was concerned, Stavros, the owner of the builders' yard, had sold us defective tiles, and she was after his blood.

We skidded into his yard. She ran over and vented her anger with loud abuse, punctuated by the occasional poke in the chest to emphasise each point.

"You sold me leaking tiles," she yelled.

"I sold you the best Italian tiles that will never leak," he assured her.

"Then take them back and give me proper Greek ones," she screamed.

"Look, I will call my friend the roof guy. He will know how to fix the problem," he assured her.

Alex still refused to hear my proposed fix, and we arrived home to find two burly builders looking up at our new roof with a smug smile. Stavros had followed us, and was now deep in conversation with the two builders and Alex.

"Nothing wrong with the tiles," they all finally announced. "We need to take them all off and put them back properly."

Knowing my wife as I do. I knew there was no point in me contributing to the conversation. She was on a rant, and if I got too involved, the fury would be taken away from the direction of Stavros and sent to me. After all, I was the designer. So, I just watched and waited.

It was agreed. Amateurs should not attempt difficult building projects. This should have been left to the professionals. As we had made a hash of the roof, the builders would return later and do it "properly".

I waited for them to leave, took out my saw, and chopped a few inches off each leg, dropped the structure down and started the hose.

No leaking. It was fine.

Alex grudgingly accepted that I did really know best. But in any Greek village, any problem needs to be fully discussed and argued about first. It's just democracy in the country that invented it.

I love living here.

A delicate operation. (Part 1)

One thing I love about Greece is the lack of formality. They do not put people on a pedestal and worship them just because they happen to have a good job. Our local mayor arrives at our house for coffee on his twenty-year-old moped after cleaning out his chicken coop, and still smelling of the contents. Our local doctor spends most of his time playing backgammon in the cafe with the village priest and fishermen.

When my wife needed a cataract operation, we found a local hospital that was more than happy to book her in straight away. Alex being a little nervous about the procedure, and me being no spring chicken, and my own eyes having seen better days with cataracts beginning, I agreed to offer some moral support and have mine done too. After all, we do everything together. Why not this as well?

The day of the operation came. Alex was becoming increasingly nervous as we waited in our room. Then Fay arrived. A lovely Greek lady with rosy cheeks and a wide smile. She was our eye surgeon. She sat at the table and chatted about the local beach and recommended we pop into the nearby *taverna* for lunch after the operation. If she wasn't too busy, she would likely join us because they had the best *calamari*.

She took a quick look at our eyes, checked the notes and then asked:

"Who's first then?"

I volunteered to go first and followed Fay into the operating theatre. Alex waited just outside. My procedure lasted only ten minutes before they wheeled me out into the recovery area next door.

Alex was next. I watched from one eye as she disappeared into the theatre. A few moments later, I heard gales of laughter from inside. Fay was telling Alex jokes to put her at her ease. Alex responded by doing the same, and the laughter spread to the nurses who were all joining in the festivities. It sounded like a party going on. This continued for a few more moments until I heard Fay's voice.

"Alex. For God's sake, stop making me laugh. This is a delicate operation."

More laughter erupted until things slowly went quiet. A few moments later, a still-sniggering Alex was wheeled out to the recovery area and parked beside me.

We both felt fine after a brief rest and were allowed to sit on the side of the bed.

Then Fay appeared, checked our eyes and asked, "Who's buying lunch then?"

I love living here.

A delicate operation.
(Part 2)

EYE SURGERY WITH CHEESE PIE ON THE SIDE.

We had lived with our fresh eyes for three years after our cataract surgery, when Alex noticed her eyesight was fading again. It was getting a little foggy, and she was having trouble driving at night. We were spending some time in England and didn't know any eye specialists here. Alex called Faye, our Greek eye surgeon, to ask if she had any recommendations.

"I'm here in England now. Come to the hospital and I'll have a look," she told Alex.

Faye used to work full-time at a hospital in England. After all, this is where she received her training. But although her pay was good, she has access to modern equipment and a good living standard, she missed Greece too much to stay permanently.

So, she arranged a compromise. She now works at a hospital in Greece for two weeks in every month, and the other two weeks at an English hospital. We were fortunate she was here now.

We sat in the consulting room and chatted. The subject of Alex's eyes didn't come up for ages. Fay and Alex were far too busy catching up on the gossip and discussing the best way to make *tiropita*.

Finally, Faye stood up and shone a light into one of her eyes. She sat down at her desk and switched on a plasma screen, which showed decreasing letters sized from large at the top to minuscule at the bottom.

"Read the lowest line," Faye commanded.

"I can't even read the top one," Alex replied.

"You are such a drama queen, Alex. You can see most of it, can't you?"

"Okay, I can see most of it, but not the bottom two lines," she confessed.

Faye wanted to look deeper and decided to add drops to her eyes to dilate her pupils. The last time Alex had these drops, she ran around the consulting room in pain, holding her eyes and knocking over chairs, screaming that she was blind now. Faye remembered her naughty patient from her last visit.

"You know it is going to sting a little," she warned. "I don't want you to make a fuss like you did last time."

Alex put her head back and allowed the drops. Suddenly, the sting came.

"Stamping your feet on the floor while holding your head and yelling 'Oh my God, I'm completely blind now' will not take away the sting, Alex. You are such a baby," Fay said.

Once Alex stopped complaining, Fay used her machine to look deeply into her eyes. She diagnosed a minor issue with the surface of the eye over the lenses, which could easily be corrected with a quick laser treatment.

We arranged to meet again the next day to have the treatment. Faye assured her it was a simple, painless procedure.

The next day, we arrived with a freshly baked cheese pie and a *baklava*. In Greece, you never visit a friend without a gift. Why should England be any different?

First were the dreaded drops to dilate Alex's pupils.

"Peter, hold her head," Fay told me.

Putting Alex in a headlock, I held on tight. She was lying across two chairs, wriggling and yelling with her legs kicking into the air while Faye quickly administered the drops. As the sting subsided, Alex calmed down. We waited for them to take effect and the treatment began.

"That's the first eye done," Faye announced.

"Thank you, Fay, that was great. I didn't feel anything."

"Don't thank me yet. It doesn't always work the first time," Fay grinned.

"But I can see," Alex replied.

"Okay, you can thank me now then," Fay smiled.

The other eye was soon done, and we all sat in her office, each with a handful of cheese pie, munching happily while patients waited on a row of chairs outside for their turn. They must have heard the loud laughing through mouths full of cheese pie and were now looking forward to joining in the fun.

Alex and Fay brought informality to the most austere place. This is how all hospital appointments should be.

Only Greeks could combine lunch with eye surgery and turn it into a social event.

Independence Day.

The last few weeks have been a struggle, but a happy one. I just finished my new book. Alex broke the habit of a lifetime and read the manuscript. There were a few artistic differences, but we compromised. My bandages come off tomorrow, and they should take the stitches out next week.

Wow, she is such a patriot. Let's remember Greek Independence Day on March 25th, and celebrate this special occasion with all of our Greek friends.

Happy Independence Day to all.

The wonderful traditions of my Greece.

Easter, the most important period in the Greek calendar is coming. It's a time full of different rituals that allows us to mourn the loss of Jesus Christ and to contemplate his life, and celebrate his rebirth. This religious festival ends on Easter Sunday with the celebration of rebirth. So, after a long fast, we eat lamb.

When was the last time you saw an animal carcass hanging on a hook in the butcher's shop window?

The only relationship with meat most of us have is the little polystyrene trays with cling film stretched over an appetising slice of steak in the local supermarket, or a portion of chicken McNuggets from the local drive-through. This is an effort to disguise or somehow sanitise the meat-eating experience.

But not in Greece.

This is the time of the traditional Easter Sunday lamb roast. A visit to the local supermarket on Easter Saturday is eye-opening. Shoppers with lamb legs sticking out of their trolleys complete the Easter shopping. Whole bodies with the head still attached are curled around bottles of wine and bags of strange-looking offal ready to be made into the *kokoretsi*.

Most families will spit-roast their own whole lamb, or a goat over a bed of charcoal with all the trimmings. During this time. A mist of sweet-smelling smoke that hovers over the village invades your senses, emanating from hundreds of individual barbecues, all turning a whole animal over a bed of hot charcoal. The entire family is involved in the cooking, with everyone taking their turn to wind the spit.

Families who don't have a garden to cook a lamb in will go to the local *taverna*. The restaurant will not try to hide the reality of the food. They proudly display a poster next to the turning lambs. It's a cute picture of a sheepdog holding a bottle and feeding a lamb while its brother is turning on a spit together with another containing *kokoretsi*, the inside bits wrapped in intestines.

In Greece, you know what you're eating. If you need reminding, just look up at the cute picture. This is a wonderful tradition that will never die, and nor should it.

Scary boat cover.

It's the time of year to take the boat out. It's been sitting on its trailer next to my house covered in a tarpaulin and waiting for spring to return. It's always interesting to see if it still works after sitting motionless for the entire winter, but by far the biggest challenge is removing the cover.

The boat is over thirty-five years old, only around 4.5 metres, with an antiquated and very moody two-stroke engine. But during the winter, lots of the village wildlife have made their home in it, and are snug under the soon-to-be-removed cover.

I usually begin by sneaking around the boat and very quietly untying the holding ropes, so that the cover is just perched loosely on top of the boat.

The hidden creatures are now beginning to get suspicious. A few sleepy wasps emerge and start buzzing around my head. At this stage, if I grabbed the boat cover, I would likely have a handful of wasps' nest too. Experience from last year taught me that!

So next, I get a big stick and dance around the boat, hitting the cover and yelling at the top of my voice, making as much noise as possible hoping to scare them off, before running away and watching from a safe distance behind my shed.

The neighbours are used to this ritual, and they lean over their walls to enjoy the show. I watch, waiting for any snakes, rodents, bees or wasps to leave the boat. After a few moments, I'm disappointed to see only two wasps buzzing around.

Slowly, I walk back to the boat, take a corner of the cover, carefully lift it and peer underneath. It looks safe, so I hold the cover and run at full speed up the garden, dragging it behind me before dropping it and continuing to run.

As usual, there were a few wasps' nests glued to the cover waiting to attack, a family of mice who had made a nest in my seat cover, a small grass snake coiled up under the steering wheel, and a selection of lizards, who just scuttle over the side and disappear into the long grass. Not a bad result really.

Next, I needed to find out if it still floats.

More later.

Some people feel sorry for me.

I just got this interesting review on Goodreads. See, some people feel sorry for me. They see how I have suffered. This reviewer certainly realised what I went through.

> I'm reading this book and, for the most part, enjoying it...however, I have to rant about something. I don't think practical jokes and pranks are at all funny because they're always at the expense of someone--in this case, the author and husband. I don't find it amusing that his beloved wife tries to get him to be more open in a Greek way by embarrassing and humiliating him. But, even worse, I can't understand why he just

takes it and thinks she's improving him! If that was me, it would be more like WWIII in our house, and I'd be absolutely furious with my (darling!) hubby for hanging me out to dry and finding it funny. I just can't enjoy and find this at all entertaining and it's beyond me why and how Peter Barber finds this acceptable and a learning experience rather than an insult.

Okay, well he wasn't married at the time but, for me, nothing changed before or after their marriage. and, while I enjoyed reading about Greece, I really could barely stand to read about how his hot-tempered gf/wife didn't change throughout (example: the chapter re Hydra--the way she ignored his intense discomfort and later laughed about his biking was just appalling and offensive to me--and yet, how he accepted it completely with no resistance or demands they leave the island earlier was indicative of his submissive response to what I consider to be abusive behaviour).

I hope Alex reads this.
But in reality, I loved every moment of my

introduction to Greek life and culture. My life was filled with laughter and adventure, and I was treated with love and respect by my new Greek family.

If I had to do it all again, I would change nothing.

Greeks obey rules. (Eventually.)

Many Greeks still smoke. I gave up a few years ago (five years, six months, fourteen days, and eight hours ago) and hardly miss it at all. (Only every waking moment and sometimes when I'm asleep.)

When I did smoke, my lifestyle was so unhealthy that the only exercise I got was coughing. But now I've changed. After kicking my two packets-a-day addiction, I moved on to healthier pastimes, which mostly involve eating. Replacing my strict exercise regime from coughing to chewing.

A few years back, the European Union banned smoking in enclosed spaces. Greece, like other countries, needed to comply. So, they fully complied with the new law by sticking large, red, "No Smoking" signs to windows and doors of all *tavernas*, coffee bars and restaurants. Perspex "No Smoking" signs popped up on every table, usually next to the ashtray, but they still had no problem with letting people puff away happily.

The tobacco police had to take action. So, raids were in order. Mob-handed, they would swoop into a *taverna*, issue fines to anyone smoking, and double fines for the *taverna* owner. Soon the ashtrays were removed from the tables and stored away. If you wanted to smoke, you had to ask for one. Slowly but surely, the *tavernas* were fined into submission. The law was finally working. But that was in Athens!

The islands and villages are a different matter. It's not cost-effective to patrol outlying villages and islands. These are close communities that stick together. If one *taverna* is raided, then the word spreads to all others in the region to hide ashtrays and look innocent. The unlucky officials then get bored and go away.

In one of my favourite fish *tavernas* near my house, the owner gave up smoking a couple of years back. But he always has an unlit cigarette in his mouth to remind him of his lost love. He doesn't judge others. All of his clients are free to smoke. It's always been that way, so why change now?

My brother, who still has the disgusting and unsociable habit, (ex-smoker's "Holier than thou" comment) was surprised when he got up from the table in a local *taverna* to go outside for a smoke. The owner pulled him back to the table and put an ashtray in front of him. He was delighted. He will certainly spend all of his future holidays in Greece, thus boosting the economy.

Greece has among the toughest anti-smoking laws in Europe, but it has never been implemented. According to the latest Euro barometer survey on smoking in May 2017, eighty-seven per cent of Greeks said they have come across people smoking in bars and seventy-eight per cent in restaurants—compared to the European Union average of twenty per cent and nine per cent, respectively.

Greeks obey rules, (eventually), but they must make sense to them. Until then, it's freedom for all. Including smokers.

April

IN OUR GREEK VILLAGE

The weather warning.

Issued on Friday for the morning of Saturday 1st of April. Vast amounts of heavy rain and strong winds were expected, from early in the morning. A shower of small fish has already been reported in Corinth, and a hailstorm of frogs in Glyfada. The residents of Glyfada have already lodged a complaint to Corinth, stating it's not fair. They get all the best weather.

Happy weekend my friends!

Hissssss...

My sister arrived at our home in Pefki last night. We are having a family Easter, and we will join her soon.

Gill arrived at night, and the house was dark. As she stepped out of the car, our neighbour who had heard her arrive came over.

"Welcome. But beware of snakes, they are everywhere," he warned.

Gill switched her phone light on and scanned the ground. She picked her way up the stairs to the entrance, listening for the hiss of snakes, or a rustle from the ground, and entered the safety of the house.

This morning I received a phone call.

"There's an enormous snake in your tree," she yelled down the phone. "I've been sitting here watching it for an hour. It hasn't moved yet. I don't want to go inside in case it follows me."

"Don't move," I told her. "I know that snake, he's really ferocious. If you step away, he will chase you."

I wonder how long it will take her to realise that it's my rubber snake. It's been up that tree for years.

After all, it is April 1st.

Just a little gardening.

At our home in Evia, we have a lovely lady, Maria, who takes care of our home while we are away. As we are returning soon with family and friends to celebrate Easter, I asked her to arrange a little preparation.

"Can you ask Nikos to cut the lawn before we get there?" I asked.

"No, there are too many snakes this time of the year. It would not be a good idea to take the lawnmower out yet," she replied.

"Can't he wear wellies?" I asked. I really wanted the garden to look nice for when everyone arrives.

"I know. I have an idea. He can use his bulldozer," she told me.

"You can't use a bulldozer on my grass," I complained. "It's taken years to get a nice lawn. If you bulldoze it, all that would be left would be bare earth and I will have to start again and grow a new one."

Then I suddenly realised. It's the first of April.

I laughed down the phone. "You got me, Maria. I fell for that April Fool's joke. Well done."

"What's April Fool?" she asked.

Shopping in our Greek village.

In our sleepy Greek village, we don't bother with the internet. Home shopping is not a new concept here.

High streets of the world are fast becoming a ghetto of takeaways and betting shops. Even the larger chain stores are suffering and one by one closing their doors. This is because millions of people all over the world have changed their habits. They sit with phone in hand, scroll through the shopping sites, and click. The next day, the purchase arrives, nicely wrapped and delivered to their door.

In our Greek village, we don't need all that. Here, the shops come to us.

Yesterday, the village boutique arrived outside

our house. The vendor assured us he was selling the latest fashion straight from the catwalks of Paris. It must have taken a while to get here – most of the clothes seemed to be retro throwbacks to the nineteen fifties. But I did like the red dress.

The fishmonger came with a selection of fish straight from the harbour. They were certainly fresh. An octopus tried to bite me as I was choosing it for lunch.

The mobile pet shop does a roaring trade with sales of chickens and rabbits. But strangely, I rarely see them running around local gardens. They seem to disappear rather too quickly. But the village does have a delightful smell of roasting meat and casseroles from the outside wood ovens.

A truck arrived piled high with emerald-green watermelons cut from the field this morning. Watermelons in our village are huge. All the best ones are sold locally, mainly because the only way to get it from the truck to your house is with a wheelbarrow. So, if you wanted to buy one this big in a supermarket, you would need a van and a forklift to get the shopping home.

Vans and trucks drive slowly around the village. Some sell chairs and patio sets. Others contain enormous varieties of potted plants, trees and fresh flowers.

Even the local shepherd gets in on the bounty. He always seems to have fewer goats when he leaves the village than when he arrived.

Then, when you have acquired more stuff than you really need, the *paliatzis* (scrap merchant) arrives to take away any junk you don't need any more.

So, no, we don't need Amazon Prime here. We still like to shop the old way.

The Greek sun is sneaky.

We arrived in Greece mid-April for Easter. The weather was still spring-like, the heat of summer still a month or two away. But the Greek sun is sneaky and lulls you into a false sense of security.

"Come, sit down, let me warm your face," it assures you. Then when you are not looking, it creeps up and cooks the meat off your bones.

We had arranged to have lunch with a few friends and booked a table at a seaside fish *taverna*. The restaurant was busy, our party was large, so we couldn't all fit round a table in the shade, so, as it was not too hot, and the sunshine was pleasantly warm, we sat in the sun to eat.

In Greece, lunch will usually last four to five hours, and I had fallen into that trap. Straight off the plane from cold, damp London, sitting in the warm sun, was a blessed relief after a grey winter. But the Greek sun was about to claim yet another stupid Englishman. I should have known better. After all, I have mostly lived here for over twenty years. But the local Greek wine was obviously in cahoots with the sun and assured me everything was fine and not to worry, so feeling happy in the warmth of the sun, fine Greek food, lovely company, all was good with the world, but unknown to me, I was being slowly roasted.

I awoke the next day. My face burned. It had done pink, gone straight past red, and overnight had turned purple with water-filled blisters on my nose and forehead. My naturally pink skin had changed, leaving me looking like a flashing beacon. I suspected I was glowing in the dark. Being a blonde, pink person, I could never get a golden tan.

Alex, being Greek with olive skin, only needs to step out of the house to go three shades darker. I just go redder until it all peels off and the process starts all over again. I live my life in the summer with a permanently peeling red, blotchy nose.

If I'm not scratching mosquito bites, I'm clawing away at prickly heat, which gives me constant rashes up both arms. Before I leave the house, Alex makes me stand naked in the living room while she plasters me with a factor fifty sunblock, then adds nappy rash cream to my little creases to protect me even further. It is always embarrassing, but in Greece, in the summer, it is the only way to survive.

Therefore, I wear hats. My normal hat supplier is the local tourist shop. For a few euros, I can get one or two, which usually last me the summer before disintegrating. But it was not tourist season yet. The only hat available was my pet hate: baseball caps. So, I rummaged around at home and found some of Alex's. I particularly liked the green one.

Luckily, the villagers all know me and I just smile as I say good morning from under my green floppy hat with dandruff from my peeling face raining onto my dark T-shirt. They just smile back and walk away, shaking their heads.

All you lovely people coming to Greece for your holidays. Take note. Wear a hat. Head and shoulders shampoo doesn't help with dandruff from a peeling face.

Will I ever learn?

Beware!! In Greece, shopping can get you drunk.

Greek *kiosks* (περίπτερο) are everywhere. These micro shops sit on almost every corner in Athens and all major cities. My island village has two. They sell almost everything. From cigarettes to milk, beer, confectionery, ice cream and tourist memorabilia. They are little Tardises full of interesting merchandise and they never seem to close.

As well as being shops, they also sell bus tickets, phone cards, and give directions to anyone who asks, and call taxis. They are an important part of life in Greece and essential to the community.

There is one on the main road from Glyfada, near Athens, which is quite exceptional. This was the world's first drive-through.

You just pull your car near to the window, yell your order over the noise of the passing traffic, and a shovel comes out of the *kiosk*. You deposit your money under a clip, and they pull the shovel back before poking it back into your car window with your change and goods. I think most of the multinationals got the idea from that one little *kiosk* near Glyfada.

Near our village in North Evia, my sister asked me to stop the car while she went into our local *kiosk*. She wanted to buy some soft drinks and needed directions to a local butcher's shop. Unknown to me, she was planning to cook a nice barbecue for us that evening, but it would be a surprise.

After fifteen minutes, she hadn't returned. I left the car to search for her. There she was, sitting on an old wooden chair inside the *kiosk*, giggling with the owner and looking tipsy. He had offered her a free sample of his home-made fire water, *tsipouro*. So, she had forgotten about the soft drinks and was comfortable passing the afternoon boozing with the old man in his *kiosk*.

I left them to it and didn't see her for the

rest of the afternoon. She returned home early evening looking slightly drunk with a bag of shopping and a smile.

She had found the butcher's, but because of the heat, Greek butchers will not have meat on display, so you must ask for what you want. My sister didn't speak a word of Greek, but had heard stories of some Greek foods, mostly involving the inside bits of animals that she didn't fancy. The butcher didn't understand English, so the dance began. After strutting around the shop making chicken noises and mooing sounds, everyone in the shop was laughing, but no meat was being produced. So finally, she asked for a pen and paper and drew a diagram.

She passed a picture of a penis and testicles to the butcher with a cross through the drawing, and said, "Anything but that."

The butcher understood, and to thank her for the entertainment, insisted she join him for a glass or two of *tsipouro* before selling her a few lamb chops. She had really enjoyed the afternoon but was now too drunk to cook. We had sandwiches that day.

Tourists be aware. Shopping in Greek villages can be great fun, but you probably need to be carried home.

The way home.

Another great day spent travelling through Greece. We left our hotel near Mount Olympus after breakfast and drove around the perimeter on our way south to our home in Pefki, Evia. We stopped on the motorway for fuel and a coffee. Alex chewed thoughtfully on a cheese pie and made a suggestion.

"Let's go to Trikeri first."

We often sat in our local fish restaurant near our home in Pefki, looking across the Straits of Artemis at the tiny white buildings perched on the top of the mountain. Now was our chance to go. OK, it was over four hours out of our way, but why not?

I don't mind driving, but travelling with

Alex is difficult and time-consuming. She loves to take photographs of anything beautiful. In Greece the mountains are spectacular, and the sea is amazing, everywhere you look is worth photographing. So, our four-hour drive became seven hours with cries of "Stop, stop, stop!" every time we saw a fishing boat, hill, river or cat. Not content to snap from the car, I must stop while she wanders around photographing anything interesting.

We finally arrived at our destination after photographing every stretch of seashore, all the mountains of Pelion, twenty-three flocks of goats and every interesting fishing boat in the bay of Volos.

Trikeri looks lovely from a distance, but even more beautiful when you arrive. Built on top of the southernmost point of the Pelion mountains, the view of the Bay of Artemis is incredible, but scary.

The village streets were originally built to allow two donkeys to pass each other without one falling off the mountain, but certainly not wide enough for a large SUV driving around sightseeing. I soon realised it was a bad idea when we turned into a narrow-cobbled road towards the interior of the village and found there was nowhere to reverse. To get out, we needed to drive all the way around the village, negotiating left and right turns, around the side of the mountain peak, through gaps in between buildings with only millimetres to spare. Alex leaned out of one window, making sure we didn't scrape the rows of white buildings; I hung out of my side, ensuring the front wheels didn't slide off the road. With a sheer drop off the cliff edge, that would certainly have spoiled our day. After half an hour of terror, we thankfully emerged onto the main road.

Now, I'm sitting in the local *taverna* in my village, sipping a coffee, writing this account while looking across the calm Aegean at the beautiful village of Trikeri shining in the morning sun like a cluster of white sugar lumps perched on the mountain. But after all the years of seeing it across the sea, I can now say we have been.

I'm not going there again.

A lovely day in the village.

Yesterday, we had lunch at our favourite fish *taverna* near our home. Easter is almost upon us, so the food available is restricted to "fasting food," *calamari*, lentils and salads.

One minor problem is we have my brother and his wife staying with us at the moment, and they don't eat fish.

Mr Balaroras came and sat at our table to take the order. Alex asked if he had anything less fishy for Jon and his wife.

"Don't worry, I will cook octopus for them. That's not fish."

Jon wrinkled his nose.

"Okay, shrimps?" he suggested.

"Do you have any pork chops?" Alex asked.

"Alexandra, this is a fish restaurant." He was getting angry now. "If you wanted meat, you should have called me. I would have called the butcher, he would have delivered, then I could have cooked it. He's closed now, so it's fish or nothing."

So, Jon and his wife ended up with a Greek salad, a plate of chips and some fried cheese while Alex and I tucked into a selection of shrimps, *calamari* and lentils.

It was a lovely meal, but as usual, we had ordered a little too much. We called for the bill. Mr Balaroras came over, took one look at the unfinished food.

"You haven't finished yet. You are not going anywhere until you have eaten everything," he said, and went back into his kitchen.

Alex took a tissue and wrapped the uneaten calamari while I packaged up the shrimps and stuffed them in my pocket. He returned, checked the table and with a shrug, said, "That's better, you can go now," and sat down to calculate our bill.

We left with pockets bulging, leaving a trail of shrimps from the *taverna* to the car.

But the cats were happy when we arrived home.

The incredible story of two Greek cats.

This is something I have never seen.

We arrived home to find one of our local stray cats had given birth to three kittens. We went along to the pet shop and got a new house and blankets for her and the kittens. We transferred them all to their new home.

Another cat arrived who was clearly pregnant and was about to give birth, so we went back to the shop and brought another house for her.

When we arrived home, the new arrival had moved in with the kittens and mother. She was giving birth to her own brood in the same box. Currently, the mother of the first batch of kittens is cleaning the offspring of the second batch, while the new mother is feeding the older kittens.

So, remarkably, we now have two nursing mothers sharing the duties of feeding and cleaning each other's kittens in the same little container.

True shared motherhood.

My wife isn't speaking today.

T his is rare. Like most Greek wives, she always has something to say. But not today.

Early this morning, she went to the local church and took Easter Holy Communion. So, she isn't allowed to swear for the whole day.

Alex descended from a long line of Greek sea captains and was immersed in salty language from an early age. This has never left her. When we first became a couple, with me being an innocent non-Greek speaking Englishman, I struggled to learn the language. Alex helped. But I soon realised the words being taught could not be found in any phrase book, or English/Greek dictionary.

A trip to the local shops to buy bread

would result in tears of laughter from the baker. I never returned to any Greek bakers after that experience. Asking the petrol pump attendant to fill me up, rather than the car, I soon realised that Alex probably wasn't the best teacher, and perhaps I needed to learn Greek elsewhere.

So today the house is strangely quiet. No loud conversations shouted from garden to garden. No squabbles with the neighbours or local tradesmen. It's going to be a peaceful day, but I suspect she's saving it up for tomorrow. I may take her to the church again tomorrow.

I love living here.

Good news!

I'm alive. Currently sitting with a coffee, a glass of fresh orange juice and calming my nerves.

Taking a ride in an Athenian taxi is an interesting experience. The first challenge is actually being permitted to get in one. It goes something like this:

Hold your hand in the air.

Taxi stops.

Driver winds down his window and asks, "Where would you like to go?"

You give the driver your destination.

He lifts his head in the Greek style and tuts.

"I'm not going anywhere near there," he informs you and drives away.

The only way you are allowed to get in a

taxi, is if your destination coincides with his. Otherwise, you are out of luck.

You must consider strategy before giving away your destination. Which direction was the taxi travelling in when you hailed him, does he look like he's in a hurry, perhaps ask where he's going first. You may get lucky.

We had to be at Piraeus in time to catch a ferry to Agistri. We couldn't be late; we had already booked and paid for the hotel, and there was only one ferry today, so we had to get to the port.

We had to try something drastic, so we formed a plan. I held up my hand, the taxi stopped, and the window was wound down to ask the usual question. But this time, while the driver was distracted, and before he had a chance to refuse, my wife Alex sneaked around the back and jumped into the seat. Without another word, I joined her. We both smiled at the driver. He smiled back, knowing we had won this first battle. But the next round was still to come.

With our backsides firmly on the seat, he had no choice. He had to drive us to the port. We were pinned back in our seats as we watched the buildings flash by in a blur. This is when he decided to show the skills learned at the kamikaze school of driving on how to deconstipate your passengers.

It worked. Round two to the taxi driver.

After an interesting trip tossed about as though sitting on a rabid dog trying to shake fleas off its back, we arrived at the port in record time. We both felt dizzy as we climbed out of the taxi and paid. The driver gave us his card and smiled.

"Whenever you need me, just call, I will be there," he assured us, disappearing in a cloud of tyre smoke to find another victim.

We boarded a long yellow cigar tube and set off. This was the Flying Dolphin. Another exciting experience. It felt like being in a diesel-smelling washing machine on legs, skimming across the sea on the spin cycle. But it was quick, and we arrived on the island in record time.

So, after our speedy morning experience, we have arrived, and everything has slowed down.

We have arrived on the beautiful island of Agistri.

More tomorrow.

Experience the real Greece.

To really appreciate the beauty of Greece, it's necessary to go a little deeper. Most people visit for the weather, beaches and history. Tourists rarely experience true Greek culture, which is a shame because it's wonderful.

As a writer, I tread a fine line between humour and unintended offence. My stories are of real-life experiences in Greece, seen through my eyes and largely around my marriage to a Greek national.

What right has a foreigner got to write about Greece?

While I was writing my recent book, *A Parthenon on Our Roof*, it soon became clear that Alex was watching me closely. I would write a draft chapter; she would read it, then throw it back at me with a few interesting Greek swear words and threats of minor violence, usually informing me it was *malaka*.

A few days later, I would rewrite the chapter and hide in the garden wearing a tin hat while she read the revised version.

Alex, like all Greeks, has a deep patriotism for her country. But she is not a nationalist. What separates patriotism from nationalism in Greece is Greek hospitality and philoxenia: love of strangers. Greeks love strangers and have an eagerness to show hospitality.

When I first came to live in Greece, like all foreigners I found it easy to criticise. Things were different here. But slowly, as I merged into Greek life, my new family adopted me as a long-lost son. I soon realised that far from being different, it was just more intense. Love was deeper. They showed genuine emotions, nothing hidden. People were truly pleased to meet me and bring me into their homes.

As a previously stuffy Englishman, this was unsettling.

I was not used to this direct approach. In England, people don't feel comfortable probing into your life and confine conversations to the weather. In Greece, anything goes. Friends will prod and poke until your shell is opened and they release your soul. At first, it was a disconcerting experience, but now it comes naturally.

Don't ask what's in it.
(Part 1)

We grew up in the late 1960s in England. In those days, my only association with Greece was watching *Jason and the Argonauts* at the local picture house. Little did I know I would become an honorary Greek when I grew up.

We all know Greek food is the best in the world. In our early years in the UK, they weaned us on simple basic food. Although nourishing, it did lack the variety found in Mediterranean countries. When I was a kid, pasta came in tins, garlic was unsociable, and we only found olive oil in pharmacies to pour into our ears, and never into salads. When I married a Greek, all of this rapidly changed.

As kids, my younger brother, Jon, was

raised with me on the same diet, but he never widened his culinary tastes. The only part of a fish he had ever eaten was a "Captain Bird's-Eye" finger. The only meat eaten has to be identifiable. A lamb chop, piece of steak, sometimes a sausage, or hamburger.

But this changed when he came to visit during Easter.

It was Easter Sunday. The church celebrations had ended and the Lent fast was behind us. We were free to eat meat again. So, we went to the local *taverna* for the traditional meal.

The first course was the traditional soup, *Magiritsa*. This is eaten to adjust your stomach to eating meat again after the long abstinence. Jon looked down at the bowl of green soup in front of him and asked Alex.

"What's this and why is it green?"

"It's made with lettuce and dill," she replied. "That's where the colour comes from."

Jon dipped his spoon into the soup. He loved it and finished the bowl.

He looked up at Alex and asked, "Was there meat in there too?"

"Yes," Alex replied. "Heart, liver, lungs, kidney, spleen and intestines."

Jon turned greener than the soup as he absorbed this information. But he had enjoyed it, so it was too late now. He was now suspicious. He pointed to the BBQ where the Easter lamb was slowly turning. Underneath was the *kokoretsi*.

"What's that?" he asked.

"It's like a Greek sausage," I replied. "You will love it."

Don't ask what's in it. (Part 2)

We were enjoying our traditional Greek Easter. The *magiritsa* soup had been eaten, and bowls cleared away. We turned our attention to the main course. My brother had been suspiciously watching the golden *kokoretsi* slowly turning on the spit. After finding out what the soup was made of, he was a little wary of the next course. The lamb looked fine, as it was clearly identifiable, but the *kokoretsi* on the next spit was a different matter.

"So, tell me exactly. What is it?" he demanded.

I really wanted to introduce him to proper Greek food. If I told the truth, he would never have tried it, so I lied.

"It's like a sausage, but instead of minced up meat, this has whole chunks of lamb," I assured him. "You will love it." I didn't explain what part of the lamb it was.

"What's it wrapped up in?" he asked.

"It's like pork crackling. But instead of pork, it's lamb," I told him.

Jon seemed satisfied and agreed to try it. A large portion was laid on the table. We took our forks and started to eat. He tried the outer coating.

"It tastes like bacon," he said as he chewed on the grilled intestines. At last, he had found something he felt comfortable eating. Then he dug a little deeper and pulled out a large spongy chunk of something.

"What's this?" he asked.

"Oh, that's a bit of spleen, or maybe heart. No, sorry, it's lung," Alex told him.

He put down his fork and refused to eat any more. It wasn't going well. Poor conservative Jon had eaten every bit of the lamb except the baa and wasn't in the mood for any more experiments.

"Can't we just have some BBQ lamb?" he pleaded.

The lamb was taken off the grill and cut into chunks, ready to be served to hungry diners. Plates of golden meat were passed around the little *taverna* until our turn came. Then the waiter put a portion in the centre of our table and placed another plate for the honoured guest in front of my brother.

It was the head.

Jon stared at the head. The head stared back and smiled.

Jon left.

A lovely day on my island.

After a full day, the Easter celebration is over. Guests have gone home. Shells of red eggs are spread around the floor, and the cats are gnawing on the bones of the Easter lamb. I feel sleepy, but content.

It was a good day which began just before midnight. The entire population of our village had assembled outside the church to await the announcement, and to share the light of resurrection. It had been a period of mourning up until now. The suffering of Christ, and the crucifixion had been remembered by fasting and quiet reflection.

But this was about to change.

The light was brought out of the church, a flame flown from Jerusalem and shared with every church in Greece. Everyone takes the light from person to person until everyone is holding a white candle with a flickering flame.

At the stroke of midnight, the priest calls out, "*Christos Anesti.*" (Christ has risen.) The man holding the rope puffs on his cigarette and enthusiastically pulls until the bells start to ring announcing the resurrection. Fireworks are set off, and the effigy of Judas is burned, and flares taken from local fishing boats are set off. Everyone in the village, friend or foe, will greet each other, hug, kiss and share the happiness felt by all.

After a few short hours of sleep, it's time to prepare the Easter feast. Most families in our village will cook a whole lamb. We always do the same. So, I spent an hour wrestling with the small beast, threading it onto the spit and tying it so it wouldn't fall off. I unwrapped the previously prepared *kokoretsi* and lit the barbecue.

Living as a Greek for over twenty years, I have become quite proficient at cooking lamb but it hasn't always been this way. My earlier attempts usually resulted in bits falling off into the flames, and an Easter meal of incinerated unidentifiable black lumps. One year I ate a lump of charcoal thinking it was meat. It tasted the same. But now the lamb looked good, there was a problem with the *kokoretsi*, however.

This is an interesting dish made from all the bits inside the lamb and wrapped up in intestines. Traditionally, it's roasted with the lamb on a separate spit. But although the lamb was cooking well, the *kokoretsi* was going black. I tried lifting it higher, away from the hot coals, but it just kept getting blacker. In the end, I wrapped it in foil and hoped for the best.

Our guests arrived. I cut the lamb into chunks and laid it on the table. It looked good and smelled wonderful. But then I unwrapped the *kokoretsi* and looked at the black shrivelled stick. I tried to cut it into slices, but the knife went blunt, so I tried a hammer.

It didn't look very appetising, but our guests were kind and enthusiastically munched away while complimenting me on how good it tasted through black teeth. I knew they were lying. Such lovely people.

The afternoon and evening passed accompanied by local Greek wine, home-made *tsipouro* and relaxing conversation.

Where have all the proper dogs gone?

We were walking around Plaka in Athens a few days ago. A place where there used to be sleepy mutts relaxing in the sun or wandering around tables seeking titbits from tourists. They were gone.

They are charming creatures with genuine characters, who win your hearts with a look. Most supermarkets would have a dozing dog near the trollies. Government departments would always have their local canine happily sleeping by the door. Greek dogs have so much to offer.

When I first arrived in Greece, the family pet was a dog called Lady. She just turned up one day and moved in. When we first built our home on a Greek island, we found a stray puppy with a broken leg. We nursed her back to health and adopted her. She became an international traveller and lived in the UK and Greece with frequent trips between both countries. Not bad for a dog from humble beginnings, but she gave us far more than we gave her.

But now, they are nowhere to be seen. It seems strange-looking pets who fit into pockets have somehow replaced these old residents of Athens.

Athens is changing. But is it for the better?

Greece is changing.

Well, it is for dogs.

Having a home in the metropolitan city of Glyfada, and another in a sleepy Island fishing village in Pefki, Evia, I see so many hilarious differences.

Recently, I left home in Glyfada for a quick walk to my local cafeteria for a coffee. I passed the upmarket shops selling designer clothes, handbags, and a shop selling dog dresses.

"What! Dog dresses in Greece?" I couldn't believe my eyes.

I stopped, walked back, and looked in the window. What the hell is that? I thought. I wondered what they would make of that in our island village.

But Pefki is changing too.

Last summer, the bars and restaurants, normally occupied by a few clients, were full to bursting. The local supermarket used to be run by an old lady who would put down her knitting to serve you. A hoard of new staff has replaced her, all running around wearing yellow matching uniforms. Music bars appeared, fish spas and upmarket shops selling designer swimming costumes are dotted along the seafront. They have confined the old men of the village to one small *kafenio* near the harbour, where politics and fish are still discussed.

But the most interesting aspect of our new-found success as a holiday resort is the dogs. The visitors have brought their own. Our local stray dog population are not sure what to make of these strange little hounds being carried in handbags. Some are secured in special shoulder straps, others on glittery leads running to keep up with their owners with their legs blurred because they are not used to walking. Our local dogs lie in the shade watching these tiny dogs scamper by.

I can see their little dog minds working. *Do I need to chase these strange creatures or run away?*

They look like dogs; they smell like dogs, but are the size of cats, so are viewed with a great deal of suspicion. Remember, in Greece, cats chase dogs. So, they just watch with interest as they pass by, but do not take the chance of chasing them in case they do indeed turn out to be cats.

One enterprising individual thought it a good idea to open a fish spa! And it was next door to the village coffeehouse where the old men of the village sat to drink coffee and gossip.

"They do what?" one old man exclaimed.

Another told the group that he had read about it in a magazine.

"People pay 10 euros to put their feet into a bucket with the fish. Then the fish eat their feet," he told them.

This made no sense to the old men of the village.

"Why would people want to have their feet eaten?" the first old man asked.

"The fish don't eat all the feet," one knowledgeable individual informed the group. "Only the bad bits."

"But how do they know what the bad bits are? Are they doctors?"

The conversation and arguments took up most of the day and ended with the old men shaking their heads and complaining about the stupidity of some people.

"We never had foot-eating fish in my day. Perhaps I could take some of the *Xenos* on my boat and they can dangle their feet over the side and pay me."

I still love living here.

Greek phrases, slogans, and profanities.

The Greek language is so interesting. So much so, now I have finished my latest Parthenon book, and am waiting for the final publication, I think I will sneak a slightly different book out before the next episode.

So many of us have struggled to learn the Greek language. For years, I was fine with ordering in restaurants, general polite conversation and generally getting by. But when Alex chats with her friends I become lost, listening to a strange mix of Greek slang, profanities and confusing expressions which can never be found in phrase books.

Alex was chatting with friends at the local

taverna. Gossip was flowing about a particularly troublesome woman in the village.

"That woman is a real *farmakglossi*," I heard Alex say.

I understand *farmako*. This is a pharmacy, or medicine. *Glossi* is mouth. So why is Alex accusing this poor woman of having a mouth full of medicine? Is she ill?

When we got home, I asked Alex to explain.

"In Greece, we sometimes use the same word for poison as medicine. So, I was calling her a poison mouth because she spreads nasty gossip around the village," she explained.

"Oh, that explains it," I said. "But you also called her a *farmakomouna*. What's that?"

Alex just laughed and told me to ask someone else.

Oh dear. I've just looked it up.

What a fabulous day in Greece!

It began watching the sunrise over the monasteries of Meteora. Now, after a two-hour drive, we have arrived in the foothills of Olympus.

In between, we have climbed four mountains to visit ancient churches and a nunnery. Met new friends and seen some of the most spectacular sights in the world.

I lost count of the steps after the first hour when I looked down into the abyss below me and had my first panic attack. I looked up, trying to see Alex and gain some sympathy, but she was just a dot in the distance, skipping up the stairs, leaving me far behind. So, with nobody to feel sorry for me, I trudged the rest of the way up.

Coming down was an absolute pleasure. No more puffing and wheezing, no more straining to coax my tired legs to climb just one more step. *I'd done it!* We could get back in the car, drive down the mountain, enjoy a leisurely coffee and I could pat myself on the back.

That was until Alex caught up with me and pointed to the next monastery, which was even higher.

"We'll go up to that one next," she told me.

Tired and hungry, we arrived at our charming hotel. It's in a small village surrounded by snow-covered mountains smelling of grilled meat and wood smoke. The peaks of Mount Olympus are hidden by a blanket of cloud, adding to the legend of the twelve gods who live there. I would rather not see the top of the mountain. It's much better to imagine Zeus and the other gods sitting on thrones in their own temple above the clouds, weaving the destiny of us mortals.

But time to eat. The hotel restaurant was tastefully decorated. Jars of home-made preserves and liquors were arranged on display shelves. A log fire was roaring, and the food rivalled the best French or Italian cuisine. Wild boar casserole, Greek-style beef in tomato sauce, and elegant salads. We had to remind ourselves we were still in Greece and hadn't been transported to the French Alps.

We were reassured of our location when the owner dragged a refrigerator into the centre of the restaurant, opened a tin of paint and happily applied two coats of white gloss between serving drinks.

I love Greece.

Back in our room, Alex was staring out of the window at the cloudy mountain. She opened her mouth to speak. Before she uttered the first word, I took over.

"I know what you are going to say. The answer is no. I am not climbing that mountain."

May

IN OUR GREEK VILLAGE

Another hot day in our village

Jack Sprat could eat no fat,
His wife could eat no lean.
And so between them both, you see,
They licked the platter clean.

Alex and I are from different backgrounds. I am used to interesting weather. Usually wet, cloudy grey days, Alex is more used to the long hot summers of Greece.

Greece is a beautiful, warm, welcoming country, well suited for relaxing on the beach sipping an icy drink, with the occasional dip in the sea to cool off.

But for me, Greece is not suited to anything energetic. A short walk for a morning coffee can be a challenge. I leave my air-conditioned home and emerge into the warm air. After twenty metres, I start to sweat and reduce my pace. As I turn the corner, the sun hits me like I've walked into a wall. By the time I get to the shade of the cafe, my hair is pasted to my head, my T-shirt is wet. I feel like I have walked through a sauna where some enthusiast has thrown a bucket of water on the coals.

As a blond, blue-eyed, pink person, I am not used to this kind of heat. So, when the printers delivered two pallets of books and left them in the driveway, I was worried this could finish me. One by one, I unloaded each box and carried it to the cellar until the pallets were empty. I had changed colour from my usual tourist red to a deep shade of purple. But I was not done. I still had the packaging to deal with. The plastic had wrapped itself around a nearby tree and bits of cardboard were blowing up and down the street. The temperature was nudging forty-two degrees Celsius. I couldn't move another inch. Help was needed.

I called Alex. She skipped around, picking up the debris. She then went back to the terrace for her third online Zumba session of the day.

Alex never stops. Her energy is unnatural. She is constantly buzzing around the home, mopping, cleaning, and rearranging furniture. Unaffected by the heat, she spends hours in the garden under the full Greek sunshine, painting trees or carting plant pots from one location to another, before breaking off for her regular dance classes. She never looks tired or breaks into a sweat.

But when Alex and I come to our home in England, she shuts down. If the temperature dips below twenty degrees, she puts her coat on and refuses to move. I will happily spend all day in the garden in a T-shirt, with limitless energy, while Alex will watch from the window, shivering in a ski jacket and bobble hat, her teeth chattering.

One day, I may acclimatise to Greek summers, but after twenty years here, I'm still waiting. Meanwhile, I'm off to cut the grass. Only an Englishman is stupid enough to plant a two-acre lawn in Greece.

Octopus-flavoured doughnuts.

Yesterday evening we visited our dear friends and neighbours George and Helen, who were having an informal gathering. It was so lovely sitting in their garden with a few coffees and relaxed company. Friends discussed Greek music as some stood up to dance to emphasise the depth of feeling, giving the dance extra meaning.

Suddenly, Alex remembered we had an appointment in the village.

"We're late," she told us. "We must eat *loukamathas*. We promised. Who's coming with us?"

Earlier that day, we had lunch at a fish *taverna* near the harbour. Antonia runs it with her son Nikos, and her husband has a fishing boat to supply the kitchen. We finished our lunch and said goodbye.

"You come at ten this evening," Antonia demanded. "I want to eat *loukamathas* and I don't want to eat them alone. Christos next door makes the best ones on the island. We can go there."

"It's a kind offer, but we have to cut down our eating," Alex protested.

The enormous meals and four-hour lunches in the village were taking their toll, and we no longer walked but waddled like ducks. We had to reduce our calorie intake, but little chance in this village.

A disappointed look came over Antonia's face. Not wishing to make her sad, we agreed to increase our waist size a little more. After all, it was all in the interest of good village relations.

So, a few friends joined us, while others stayed at George and Helen's as we piled into the car for the short drive to the harbour.

At ten thirty, we arrived and took our seats as enormous plates of golden fried *loukamathas* covered with sticky local honey, cream and dollops of ice cream arrived. Some locals passing by smelled the cooking and sat at the table to join us. More chairs were added as the circle of friends increased in size, until there was a crowd of us, all with honey and tears of laughter running down our faces.

They were delicious, as was the company. We finished and sat back, holding our extended bellies, feeling a little guilty. We were just about to leave when Antonia made a suggestion.

"You know what goes really well with *loukamathas*?" she said. "Grilled octopus."

The table erupted with laughter. I thought she was joking until, at the top of her voice, she yelled, "Nikos! Throw some octopus on the grill."

We all got up from our chairs and moved to Antonia's fish *taverna* next door, where Nikos appeared with trays full of steaming octopus fresh from the charcoal accompanied by *tzatziki*, bowls of pasta covered with melted cheese, several loaves of freshly baked bread straight from the wood-fired oven, and mini bottles of *ouzo* with buckets of ice to wash it down. They invited a few tourists wandering by to join us. They turned the music up and we ate, chatting in a mixture of Greek, English, Dutch, Slovenian and Romanian. Somehow we all understood each other as we sipped *ouzo* with old and new friends long into the night.

The sky lightened over the distant mountains, announcing dawn was not far away.

Overnight, the village became smaller as the size of our family increased.

This is Greece, the home of true philoxenia, where everyone, including strangers, are genuinely welcome. If you are passing Pefki soon, *loukamathas* are on us.

Lost in translation.

Alex and I were wandering through Glyfada and came upon a local restaurant with a blackboard outside. It had a picture of the British flag and announced: "British fish and chips today."

This enterprising *taverna* owner was looking to tempt in the visiting Brits with this traditional dish. So we went in and ordered it. It delighted the owner that his advertising campaign had resulted in some clients and he disappeared into the kitchen to prepare the food. Shortly, he emerged carrying a tray and proudly laid our food in front of us and stood back, waiting for us to admire his culinary skills.

On the plate in front of us was a delicious-looking piece of fish with golden batter which looked to be cooked to perfection. But, on top of the fish, and filling the rest of the plate to overflowing, was a large helping of salt and vinegar crisps.

In Greece, chips are crisps, not fried potatoes. A simple mistake and a literal translation. The owner looked confused when we pointed this out, but was happy to listen to our advice. I didn't mention the missing mushy peas and pickled onion; I thought that may be too much information.

Greeks are more literal in naming food. I remember when Alex and I went for a meal in a traditional country pub in England. It didn't start well. On the table in front of us was a large bowl of pork scratchings. Alex picked one up and examined it.

"This snack has got hairs," she pointed. "and look, this one has a nipple."

Then she picked up the menu which included "Toad in the hole."

Alex screwed up her face while reading the offerings.

"Do they use real toads?" she asked. "I'm not eating that."

I explained that they certainly were not real toads, but she had already moved her finger to the next item on the menu. "Welsh rarebit, with bubble and squeak." I translated, and we finally ordered.

Then the dessert menu arrived. First on the list was Spotted Dick.

"I am definitely not eating that."

Translation of English food:

Pork scratchings: fried pig skin.

Toad in the hole: British sausages in a savoury pudding of flour and eggs.

Welsh rarebit: cheese on toast.

Bubble and squeak: mashed potatoes and fried vegetables.

Spotted Dick: don't ask.

A simple story of life in my Greek village.

When was the last time you met your neighbour? In many countries, we have become reclusive and hide behind our locked doors, shutting away the outside world. Sometimes you are lucky enough to receive a quick nod if you meet a neighbour taking the bins out or rushing to his car. The art of communication is fast disappearing.

But not in my Greek village. Privacy is unknown. Here, everyone knows everyone, and us being foreign is interesting. They consider us to be strange and exotic.

During an average day, we have a constant stream of neighbours passing by. The coffee pot is never cold as we listen with interest to how many fish Stavros caught this morning. Detailed information on the latest relationships is happily shared whilst probing us for information which can then be spread around the village.

We recently went to the church to celebrate the Easter service. Being a special occasion, everyone in the village was there and there was standing room only. It was such a beautiful church; I wanted to take a few photographs to remember the experience. But I wasn't sure if I would cause any offence. So, I sneakily took my phone from my pocket, held it at waist height, and glanced around to see if there was anyone looking.

Nobody was watching the priest. All eyes were on me, even the priest's. I slowly put my phone back into my pocket and smiled at the congregation. Most smiled back, and a few nodded at me.

I don't think anyone actually took offence at my trying to photograph the service. They were just keen to see what I was going to do next. Whatever it was, it would be interesting!

I love living here.

Dentist chairs and sticky cake windows.

We descended the long, pedestrianised street from the parliament building towards Monastiraki.

The centre of the street was full of small market stalls, street performers, and bands of musicians, some of them playing traditional Greek music, others playing classical music on violins. An old man pushing a brightly coloured barrel organ on wheels passed us while turning the handle and singing out of tune in a reedy voice. It was a fantastic and entertaining mix.

At the base of the hill stood the small monastery, literally Monastiraki, from which the area took its name. Alex ducked through the small doorway to light a candle and reappeared a moment later.

This is where the cake and ice cream shops are located. It always takes ages to pass these. Alex always lingers with her nose pressed against each window, looking at the sticky and creamy display while dribbling. I'm sure I saw her lick the window once.

Crossing the road to the main square outside the station, we lingered to admire the performance of a school choir, that had set up outside the station entrance. This was the central point between Monastiraki and the old town of Plaka.

We turned right into a warren of pedestrian passages leading towards the flea market. These were too narrow for any vehicle bigger than a bicycle, and the closeness of the shops made it superb for browsing. The shops were tourist-oriented and sold everything from traditional Greek cotton dresses and local football shirts to copies of classical statues, pots and vases.

In between were antique stores, each with its own theme. One specialised in old dentists' chairs, complete with pedal-operated drills. My teeth ached even at the thought of going near one of those instruments of torture; who would buy one, I wondered, and what for?

They obviously sold some, as the shop had been here for years.

In a little square nearby, army-surplus stores were filled with all kinds of collectables, including old swords and broken guns, Nazi helmets, medals and Victorian cannons. One shop had a machine gun on a tripod for sale next to a table piled with Second World War hand grenades.

At the flea market itself, the wares were spread out on the ground on lining sheets or tarpaulins and we had to be careful where we trod. Goods seemed mainly to comprise thrown-away items that people had picked out of dustbins and were hoping to sell on. It was an interesting variety, and they seemed to be doing a brisk trade.

If you plan to visit Athens soon, then don't forget your trip to Monastiraki.

Karpouzi – refreshes the parts other fruits cannot reach.

Watermelon is a unique fruit. Not only is it delicious on a hot Greek day, but it also refreshes your ears. Many times I have enjoyed a slice of fabulous Greek watermelon with juice running down my chin and dripping off my earlobes.

But in the *tavernas,* they realised that some tourists were avoiding this sweet, thirst-quenching fruit because of the wet-ear problem, so they now provide knives and forks to enable customers to cut the huge wedge into manageable portions. We traditionalists still prefer the old way.

My brother Jon and his wife, Angie, came

for a holiday at our home in Pefki. I cut them a slab of watermelon each. They had never tried it before but recognised it. They had seen the small sad specimens on the shelves in their local supermarket in the UK, which never looked very appetising so were avoided. But these were Greek watermelons. Giant, sweet, dripping portions requiring two hands to hold each slice. Angie looked at the pink flesh.

"How do they get the seeds in there?" she asked.

She had assumed these enormous fruits were far too big to grow on a tree, so must be produced in a factory and pips deliberately added.

"Oh yes," I replied. "It's a specialised art. People study for years learning how to stuff seeds in there. They add those for contrast. The melon is soft, so you need a little crunch to make it more interesting. They pack the seeds with nutrients, and they also have healthy fatty acids, like omega-3."

She seemed satisfied with my explanation and continued to bathe her ears in sticky juice while crunching on the seeds.

Greek watermelon has a variety of uses. My mother-in-law would make *glykos karpouzi,* watermelon rind preserve (spoon sweet). Some areas of Greece distil it into watermelon liqueur. I have also tried watermelon wine, which is light and refreshing. Alex's mother would chop one up and serve it in a plastic washing-up bowl.

But there is nothing like sitting in the Greek sunshine with a giant slice fresh from the fridge, eating as nature intended with a happy wet face and dripping ears.

It's Eurovision Song Contest time again.

The Greek entry is looking good, they always put on a great show. Get the popcorn out and prepare for a cultural feast.

Although the British entry didn't get any points last year, we live in hope. A couple of years ago we did OK. We came in at a respectable fourteenth place, but it was won by the Austrian bearded lady singing about a bird. RESULT!

I look forward every year to this contest as it is a real eye-opening showcase of European talent.

Previous winners include:

The Portuguese entry who sang in a high voice while trying to catch butterflies, with his sister lurking behind stroking him in a weird way.

Ukraine presented Verka Serduchka who dressed in tin foil with a windmill on his head, didn't win in 2007, but did manage second place.

Ruslana went one better when she shocked and delighted the men of Europe with her 2004 entry: "Wild Dance", performed wearing a very short skirt.

The entry that didn't win, but should have, was the Polish entry about milkmaids announcing that they were Slavic. Nobody actually took any notice of the song, but twenty million European men were sitting on the edge of their seats waiting for a "wardrobe malfunction".

Over the years there has been controversy during the performances.

Like when a Romanian singing vampire was disqualified after biting the Moldavian fairy wearing a pointy hat and riding a unicycle.

The singing turkey from Ireland was plucked and stuffed and put in the oven even before he finished his song. It was an easy mistake, as he was already wrapped in tinfoil.

The Russian entry didn't go too well as their entry was a grandma tap-dancing while knitting, but halfway through the performance she dropped a stitch and was deported to a *Gulag*.

The women wearing the big sequined evening dresses were complaining that the special effects were being overdone as the dry ice was getting under their skirts and they were getting frostbite on male bits.

The clown playing a barrel organ was disqualified after the handle fell off, and Finland's entry of a band of monsters playing loud music badly was thrown off stage for eating the tap-dancing horse so the Albanians couldn't get home.

But the voting is always true to form and fair. Cyprus and Greece gave each other the top score, twelve.

The overall winner was announced when someone dropped a cigarette on the studio cat which then ran into a box of fireworks. The judges said it was the best voice of the evening and the special effects were amazing.

I'm really looking forward to this year's contest.

Saturday rant.
HOW MUCH DO I HATE BREXIT?

Authors have really suffered. Boris Johnson hoodwinked the British people by promising more fish and blue passports, the reality of this stupidity is really taking its effect on us.

Most of the British people now realise it was a huge mistake, but not the lying, cheating, right-wing politicians who are still clinging on to the discredited confidence trick played on the people and still trying to assure us it was a good idea. Really?

Brits may not remain in Greece for over ninety days. I also must wait at passport control for an hour while my Greek wife skips through in minutes. The National Health Service is on its knees because the doctors and nurses are no longer welcome. Instead of the big red bus promising an additional 350 million a week to make the NHS better, it has ploughed through every hospital in the country, leaving chaos in its wake.

But wholesalers are also having trouble getting our books to Greece as they are mostly printed in England, and Amazon delivery from Italy, and other European countries has proved troublesome.

A lovely Greek blogger in Athens was keen to review my book. I have sent lots of books to Greece, but few arrive because of the new tariffs. So, this time, I wanted to be sure it would be delivered. I paid 50 euros to the English branch of DHL for 24-hour delivery. When the books arrived in Greece, DHL contacted the reviewer and asked for an added 55 euros to deliver. Obviously, she refused, and the book was returned.

So, enough of that, I thought. My book was conceived in Greece, written in Greece, and is about our lives in Greece. But although becoming a best seller in the UK, USA, Australia and Canada, it's not for sale in Greece.

I have found a Greek printing company. I have spoken to an Athenian distributor, contacted a few bookshops in Athens and Thessaloniki, who are happy to stock it. So, at last my book will be available in the country in which it was born.

Why? Brexit, that's why. This incredible act of self-destruction has resulted in the first country in history voting to impose economic sanctions on itself. I'm just a small-time author, so my necessary act of taking work away from British companies will make little difference. But if I am forced to take this action, what about the companies that make a difference to the economy?

Good news for Europe, bad news for Britain.

The Greek chef. Well, almost.

I love to cook. I experiment with new dishes, unsuccessfully, try new types of cakes and bake bread. I even get involved in making Greek specialities. Stuffed vine leaves, moussaka, cheese pie, I have even had a go at the Greek traditional dish of *kokoretsi*.

Flour up to my elbows, sticky cake mixes gluing my hair to my scalp, kitchen redecorated after using a high-powered food mixer: this didn't go well. I set the food mixer too high and it covered us with most of the cake as it sprayed around the kitchen and left us dripping with large fat globules from the ceiling.

Usually, the food eventually comes out OK, but in the preparation, I have left a trail of chaos behind me. Leftover entrails from the *kokoretsi* slither over the floor. Half-peeled onions litter the cutting board. The walls have changed colour to a delicate shade of textured creamy batter with more smeared over the windows. A sheep's head is kicked into the corner because I don't like that bit. Strange unidentified organs I found in the bag from the butcher holding the intestines and am not sure what to do with lay discarded in the sink while the cats watch, licking their lips.

So, in my attempt to make a nice, tasty lunch. I seem to have wrecked the house. But it's a small price to pay for my culinary creation. After all, we are all artists.

But now, after many years of marriage, Alex knows my ways and has devised a solution by following me around the house cleaning as I cook, thereby avoiding the normal disaster zone.

The only problem is that she now cleans up before I make the mess. So, by the time I have assembled all of my ingredients and tools ready to create my culinary masterpiece. I turn my back, and everything has gone.

"Did you see that knife I was going to use?"

"I washed it."

"Did you see that bit of meat I was saving to add to the souvlaki?"

"I gave it to the cats."
"Where's the yeast?"
"Back in the fridge."
"Mixing bowls?"
"Washed up and put away."

By the time I'm ready to cook, all of my carefully prepared ingredients have mysteriously vanished. Alex has reasoned that she can protect her home and save a couple of hours of work cleaning up by ensuring I get fed up with trying to find everything again, knowing I will give up and suggest going for lunch at George's *taverna* instead.

A cunning plan.

I can always cook tomorrow.

Remembering my other mother.

On this Mother's Day, I remember my wonderful mother-in-law. The Queen of Glyfada.

Some people arrive in this world and change it. Despina, Alex's mother, known to everyone as Debbie, changed lives. Her home was a place of laughter and smiles. She never got angry. She would diffuse family squabbles with a wave of her hand and her incredible logic.

Every day, she would pass endless quantities of food out of her tiny subterranean kitchen window while she continued cooking, wearing only her knickers and bra while singing at the top of her voice.

Not only was Debbie a big eater, she also

made sure that everyone around her would also eat well. From the day I met Debbie, the biggest memory of her was "large". Not just that she was a big woman, but everything she did was large.

She was also loud. Debbie never spoke softly. It was always a few decibels above the volume of a pneumatic road breaker.

Athena airport was nearby. The aircraft would take off over Glyfada. The sound of the engines would set off car alarms, rattle windows and nothing could be heard above the screeching of jet engines, except the voice of Debbie. She always surprised me she could have long conversations with a similarly loud neighbour Stella, who lived diagonally across the road and on the fourth floor of an apartment block. Debbie would yell from her kitchen and Stella would reply from way up in the air. Others along the road would join the conversation with no need to pause when a jet flew low overhead. Everyone could hear Debbie.

But when Debbie cooked, it was for an army. She had survived the war years and had experienced the famine of Athens. People died on the streets from hunger. If she had any say in the future, she would ensure that no one in her neighbourhood ever went hungry again. She would prepare the most remarkable food. Everyone knew there was always a meal at Debbie's house.

Debbie was mother to two biological children, Meno, who will be my lifelong friend. The other is Alexandra, who I am honoured to call my wife.

Debbie was also a mother to hundreds of people she met. She changed lives for the better and will be remembered with love by all who met her.

Debbie's influence was never destined to be confined to her immediate family. She had too much love to give. Everyone who met her fell under her spell. She changed lives for the better by her shining example and left this world a better place.

She will be remembered in our hearts, and pages of my books forever.

Relax, take your time. You're in Greece.

Time is an interesting concept. Einstein said that time is relative to where you are in the universe. But Greece is exceptional in the universe, it has two time zones in the same place.

If a Greek wants to meet at an exact time, they will say "English time". This means, don't be late. Greek time will suffice if you meet for a coffee or a chat. If an Englishman makes an appointment to meet at 12.00 p.m., he will normally be there waiting at 11.45 a.m. If my Greek wife makes an appointment for 12.00 p.m, she will probably arrive around 4.00 p.m.

When questioned about being late, the normal response is, "Yes? it's after 12.00 p.m. What's the problem?"

Although English are well-known time-keepers, most people in Greece run on Greek time. But there is a conflict. Greek ferries, buses and airplanes run on English time, which is most inconvenient for the average Greek.

My wife is always late. We must catch a ferry. She's still wandering around the garden in her dressing gown, watering the plants. She gives all the cushions in the house a final plump while I stand at the door jingling my keys.

I go for a walk around the garden while she moves the furniture a little, then asks my opinion of the position of the rugs on the floor.

I finally get her out of the house after she's picked a few flowers and arranged them nicely in a vase. With minutes to spare, I sit in the driver's seat and start the engine feeling a sense of relief that we would be at the port on time, when instead of getting in the car beside me, she wanders over to the neighbour for a quick chat over the wall while I sit revving the engine waiting for a quick getaway and hoping she would not accept the neighbour's offer of a quick coffee.

Finally, she's in the car, and we are on a mission. I leave tyre marks on the road as the back wheels spin, as the car speeds up, as I fly around the country roads overtaking tractors and even taxis in my hope of catching the ferry.

We finally arrive at the port to find the ferry chugging out towards the open sea while lifting the ramp, so we have to wait three hours for the next one.

Have you ever wondered why Athenian taxi drivers are such speed freaks? Their passenger is always late, the ferry will not wait, so Athens is full of yellow blurs with wheels trying to break the sound barrier. Now you know why.

We have to catch a plane to London next week.

More fun in the Greek village.

During our last visit to the UK, we found an inflatable jacuzzi in the local store and bought it. We couldn't afford a real one, and may have had a little trouble with British Airways. I only just managed to get my 3.2 metre inflatable boat and engine through last time by inadvertently leaving my toe under the scales. I didn't think I would get away with a full six-person jacuzzi with motor and flashing lights, so I settled for the economy version.

Alex decided it would look nice if we just expanded the patio a little to make a feature. This involved laying a new concrete base and paving slabs. This would be easy, as I had given

Alex a cement mixer for her birthday, so we were all set.

We went to the local merchant. Ordered the sand, cement and slabs. Started up the cement mixer, poured the contents onto the ground, and it ran away. We needed shuttering to make a frame to keep the cement in place. So we went hunting for some wood. The building material supplier didn't sell wood, so we were stuck. I didn't fancy a long drive to the main woodyard miles away. Then Alex made a suggestion.

"Let's just lay sand on the ground and put the paving slabs on top. No cement needed," she suggested.

"Brilliant!" I replied.

So, we laid the sand and the slabs on top. We took the jacuzzi out of the box and pumped it up, added water and plugged in the motor and waited for it to warm up.

A few hours later, our neighbour arrived.

"What's that?" asked Maria as she pointed at our jacuzzi sitting proudly on our newly-extended patio. She put her hand into the water and pulled it back quickly.

"It's hot," she cried as she stepped backwards away from this strange inflatable bath.

"Watch this," Alex said and pressed a button.

There was a whirring sound as the motor started, and suddenly the entire surface became a sea of bubbles. Maria stared in amazement at this strange new thing. She had already seen some strange things since we lived in the village, but putting our bath outside was a little difficult to understand. But she just shrugged her shoulders and wandered off muttering about this weird *xenos* with a bubbling bath in the garden. She couldn't wait to spread the word to the rest of the village.

That night, Alex decorated it with lights and arranged pots of flowers around it. We stood back to admire our work as there was a flash in the sky, followed by a deafening clap of thunder as the skies opened.

The rain came down in torrents. We sat under our patio roof and watched rivers form channels running down to the river at the back of our garden. Suddenly, the ground moved and our jacuzzi dropped from one side. The water emptied and added to the raging floods across our lawn. Then it righted itself and slipped down into the stormwater and floated away.

Because we had not bothered to use any

cement in the base, the sand had just washed it away, and taken our nice new jacuzzi with it.

It was last seen heading towards Skiathos. I wonder what the local fishermen will think of that strange new boat overtaking theirs. I have a feeling they will know it's mine. The word must have spread around the village by now.

The diet starts tomorrow, again.

Summer is coming. I need to get in shape for the beach. Don't misunderstand, I have no intention of showing off my muscles or kicking sand in skinny people's faces. I just would like to avoid having harpoons thrown at me this year accompanied by the call of, "Thar she blows."

Swimming near the beach, I heard a little boy complaining to his mother that it was too wavy today.

"Don't worry son, it's just the wake of that fat man swimming past!"

Then, when leaving the water, gravity takes effect. Where the rolls of belly fat aided my buoyancy in the water, allowing me to appear graceful and elegant, appearing from the sea onto dry land, I ripple back to my sun bed like an elephant seal heaving itself over the sand, casting a shadow over rows of sunbeds and being asked to stop blocking the sun by several people at a time.

I used to be able to hold my belly in. But only if I held my breath, which resulted in a blue face and bulging eyes. A small price to pay for looking slim. Now, I just get a blue face and bulging eyes with no effect on my waistline. But the most worrying part is I seem to have grown another belly. One has always been there between my chest and waist. I was fairly successful in holding that one in by not breathing. Then I grew a new belly below my old belly. What's that all about? And for some reason, I can't pull this one in, no matter how much I try. It just hangs there and wobbles.

Something has to be done.

It's not really my fault. Greek food is so delicious. I know it's the healthiest food in the world. But, when a lunch lasts four hours, chatting, sipping local wine and grazing on local specialities, then home for a quick siesta before dinner lasting another four hours, it's the culture that's to blame. It's not my fault.

So, I told Alex I had to go on a diet. We

agreed to stay away from our usual eight-hours-a-day *taverna* meals and eat at home.

"I only want salad," I told Alex.

So, the next day, I sat at the table, knife and fork in hand, ready to tuck into my lettuce leaves and slices of tomatoes, when a loaded plate was placed in front of me. It had two large pies, a mountainous pile of rice, and squeezed on the edge of the plate, a small salad.

Alex comes from her Greek mother's school of cooking. She could not conceive that I only wanted a salad. The only salad she knows is slathered with a kilo of olive oil with another kilo slab of feta on top.

"What's the problem? You have salad there, see, it's that little green thing under the pie."

So, the next day, we tried again. This time, another pile of rice, eight large meatballs with a mouth-watering aroma of garlic, smothered in tomato sauce, and a small green salad under one of the meatballs. But this time, instead of a glass of wine, she gave me black coffee, no sugar. We were getting somewhere.

So, one week into the diet I'm doing well. I haven't actually lost any weight yet. But I have developed a taste for black Greek coffee with no sugar. There's hope for me yet.

A Parthenon on Our Roof.
THE UNTOLD STORY.

You may have read in our book about our idea of building a Parthenon on our roof. What is not in the book was what happened next.

We had built our very own Parthenon. I had run afoul of the police by breaking local planning rules, which had caused quite a stir in the neighbourhood.

I thought it was most unfair to arrest me just for building a Parthenon. The last Englishman to interfere with one stole most of it. This Englishman was giving one back to Greece. There is just no pleasing some people!

In the end, I kept the Parthenon and my

freedom, but I had to remove the Delta. (The pointed bit at the front) It was too high.

So, we had our magnificent structure on our roof terrace, looking like a crown over our village. It looked fantastic looking up from the village all floodlit at night. It was beautiful. But soon we realised the downside. A little like the real Parthenon on top of the nearby Acropolis, it looks majestic perched on the hill dominating the Athens skyline, but when you actually get up close, it's nice but you don't want to spend too much time there in the full Greek sunshine.

So, we decided to put some parasols inside to protect the seating area from the sun. But Glyfada, being a seaside village, is windy. The first parasol lifted like a rocket and flew through the open roof, over the side of the terrace and disappeared. We bought another one and secured it in a bucket of concrete. The wind blew and dragged the umbrella across the terrace, taking the chairs with it, and got itself wedged between the columns. The pole broke, and the parasol launched into the sky and flew off towards the distant mountains.

We needed a Plan B.

So, we saved up some money, and employed a builder to put a roof over the Parthenon on our roof, and fit some windows and glass doors between the columns. It looked great. The Parthenon suddenly became a bedroom. We put some plug sockets and lights in, and a marble floor. We dragged our bed upstairs and Alex put up curtains and arranged flowers.

Then it rained. We stood in the middle of the bedroom, checked the windows, all dry. Looking up, the roof was dry. It was watertight. Alex left me to go downstairs to make some coffee.

"It's raining!" she yelled from downstairs.

"I know it's raining," I yelled back. "I can see it out of the window."

"No, it's raining down here," she called back.

I ran downstairs. It was indeed raining in our living room. Fat drops of water were squeezing through the ceiling, dropping out of the spotlights and running in little rivers across the floor.

When the column company built our Parthenon, they drilled into the roof to secure it but drilled straight through the roof waterproofing layer.

We looked on the bright side. Not only did we have a Parthenon on our roof, we also had an indoor swimming pool.

That was nice.

Hammock wars.

When we first built our house in our Greek island village. It was my dream to have my very own hammock. I would swing gently while Alex could peel the occasional grape and pop it into my mouth while I relaxed under the shade of the green leaves, listening to the sound of birdsong and the chatter of *tzitzikas*. I would place a table within easy reach for my beer and book and while away the days in luxury. I had originally planted two trees spaced nicely apart. Now they were ready to hold my dream between them.

I got a hammock, tied the ropes to the trees, and tried it out. Getting onto a hammock is a challenge. By the time I held it still enough to sit on, I would carefully bring my legs up one by one, then would fall off the other side. But after an hour of perseverance, I managed to get the hang of it.

Then Alex came home.

"I don't like it," she told me. "It spoils the look of the garden and blocks everything off. If anyone wants to go into the garden, they either need to limbo under the rope, or walk the long way around it. Can't you put it somewhere else?"

"But I planted the trees here," I protested. "I can't move the trees. It would take another ten years to grow more somewhere else."

"Look, if you want to relax in a tree, why not build a treehouse in one of them," she said. "Then we could just walk under you, and you wouldn't be in the way."

I didn't like where this was going. She had seen an opportunity to put me in a tree away from under her feet.

"You could take your laptop up there and write, then I could use your old writing table and put flowers there instead of those old books. It would be perfect."

"But the trees are still growing," I protested. "I would need to keep adding extra rungs to the ladder. And I might get used to it up there and revert to my ancestral heritage. I could stop shaving, learn to peel bananas with my feet, bring some friends to live there with me and live happily, exchanging tasty parasites picked off each other's bodies," I suggested, then added, "You could come too if you like. You are always telling me your ancestors were reciting poetry while mine were still living in trees. You could find out how the other half lived. It would be fun."

Alex listened to my explanation carefully.

"OK, you can keep your hammock then."

Our local fruit supplier.

Near our village in North Evia, an old man sits in front of his field on a chair beside the road. He stares into space, enjoying the day and dreaming. Beside him is a table full of local fruit and vegetables picked from his own land. A small blackboard is propped up against the tree showing today's produce. We stop the car and open the window.

"Do you have any cucumbers?" I ask.

"*Écho, écho,*" (I have, I have) he nods.

He goes back to staring into space to resume his dream.

"Can we have two kilos. please?" I ask.

I waited for him to stand up and pack my

order, but he remained seated and carried on dreaming.

"So, can I have two kilos of cucumbers," I repeated.

He looks at me and replies.

"Not yet. They are still over there in the field growing. They should be ready next week."

I love living here.

Is a million a lot?

I was looking at our book sales on Amazon. The sales figures were OK, but I was surprised to see how many people viewed it using the Prime Reading subscription.

I called my wife to take a look at the screen.

"Alex, you know that we have had almost one million page reads on our last book?"

"Is that a lot?" she asked.

"Yes," I replied, "a million is a lot."

"Is it more than a K?" she asked.

"Yes. A million is a thousand Ks and we almost have that."

Numbers have never been Alex's strong point. She is a philosopher, a writer and a highly skilled problem-solver, but when it comes to simple mathematics, she is left confused.

"So how many is a million?" she persisted.

I tried to put it into a context she could grasp.

"Look, the population of Athens is just over three million. One million is a third of that."

She still looked confused. I tried again.

"The population of Thessaloniki is less than one million, so they would all have read some of our book."

"But they mostly speak Greek, and the book is in English. "Tell me why everyone in Thessaloniki would want to read it?"

I tried again.

"Look, the big football stadium in England holds ninety thousand, so the people who have read some pages would fill it twelve times."

I was greeted with a blank look. I had run out of metaphors to explain how big a number a million was. So, I simply agreed.

"Yes, Alex. It's a lot."

I'm going to sneakily take her credit card away. If she has trouble knowing the difference between a thousand and a million, we could be in big trouble.

June
IN OUR GREEK VILLAGE

Don't trust Alex.

A friend came to visit us in the village for a few days. It was springtime, and because he was a keen gardener, he suggested we plant a vegetable patch in the garden.

When on our island, we tend not to shave every day and soon we both looked a little like hobos. I dressed in an old T-shirt and shorts, and Mike dressed in his normal tatty surgical scrubs stained from yesterday's lunch. But in the village, there is no formality or dress code, so we felt comfortable driving the short distance to the local market dressed as we were.

At the market, we browsed the stalls selling local plants, but they all seemed to be selling small watermelons, or aubergines. So, we had to ask.

My Greek is not great, and Mike's is non-existent so I called Alex.

Alex slowly and phonetically told me how to ask.

"You must ask: *Écheis agorákia?*"

I remembered the word for cucumber, *angoúri*, so it sounded right. I didn't really trust Alex, as she had got me into trouble before, but this sounded OK so I memorised the phrase.

I went to the plant vendor and in my best Greek, asked, "*Écheis agorákia?*"

The man looked at us two scruffy unshaven men. His face darkened.

"No. Go away."

*Well, that was uncharacteristically rude for a Greek! W*e moved on to the next stall and asked again. This time the vendor just shot us a withering look and turned away without replying.

Alex had played yet another trick on me. Instead of asking for a cucumber (*angoúri*) these two dirty old men had been wandering around the market asking for *agóri*. It sounded the same, but to my embarrassment meant something completely different.

We had been asking for little boys.

I decided not to buy any cucumbers that day and went home to sulk.

MUSINGS FROM A GREEK VILLAGE

But I still love living here.

Life in our village.

I lent my house to Mike for a holiday. Mike, being a well-respected doctor in England, was well up on Latin, but didn't speak a word of Greek. I had business in England, so couldn't be with him. So, I left a page of essential Greek phrases with a translation of all he needed. Top of the list: "ένα κιλό κρασί παρακαλώ." (One kilo of wine please.) He could work out the rest for himself.

The second day of his visit was his birthday. So, we called Jannis, the local *taverna* owner, and asked him to prepare a celebration meal. We gave Mike the directions and assured him he didn't need to order the food. It was all taken care of. Mike duly arrived with his family. Jannis had prepared a table decorated with flowers and started to bring out the plates of local food which we had ordered. My wife telephoned Jannis to ask if the meal was going well and was assured that everything was fine.

"You remember it's his birthday?" she asked. "Perhaps you could give him a cake to finish the meal?"

"But I don't have any cake."

"OK, but it's his birthday, so use your imagination."

An hour later, my phone rang. It was Mike. I asked him if he had enjoyed the meal.

"Yes, I loved it, but Jannis has given me a rabbit."

"Is it cooked?" I asked.

"No, alive," came the panicky reply. "What am I supposed to do with a live rabbit?"

Alex called Jannis. As he didn't have any cake, he had used his imagination as ordered and given Mike a live rabbit as a present. He suggested he could eat it tomorrow.

*Sing a song of sixpence,
a pocket full of rye.
Four and twenty
blackbirds baked in a pie.*

We woke up to a strange noise of loud chattering coming from our garden. So we went outside to find the source of the sound and there, perched on the overhead cables were hundreds of colourful birds, happily sitting and loudly squawking, having a conversation with each other.

It amazed us to see so many of these exotic birds in our garden, but we had no idea what species they were. Just then, Maria arrived from the village. She saw us staring up at the show and suggested that they were useless birds because they didn't taste very nice. Everything in the village must have a purpose. As these creatures were not very good to eat, they ignored them.

I rushed into the house, grabbed my laptop and found them on Google. They were Bee Eaters. These migratory birds had stopped off in my garden for a rest from their long journey south. I was quite pleased they were not tasty, otherwise every hunter in the village would have rushed to my garden to share in the harvest.

By the next day, they had left to continue their journey. Adonis arrived to help with the garden. He had heard about our strange fascination with these useless, inedible birds.

"I hear you like birds," he said.

"Yes, we have a bird table in our garden in England. We watch them from our window."

"So, you shoot them from your window?"

"No, we just watch them," I replied.

This made no sense to Adonis. He could not understand why we would just look at them without eating any. With that, he went out to his van and returned with a string of several dead blackbirds, all with bright yellow beaks. He laid them on the table.

"Now those are proper birds, and they are delicious."

We politely refused his generous gift. He just shrugged his shoulders and put them back in his van.

I love living here. But I don't think I will ever develop a taste for blackbirds. Even though they were once a traditional English dish.

What Greek creature bit me?

I was sitting in my garden sipping an *ouzo* and listening to the crickets playing their music. It was like a lullaby sending me gently to sleep.

I went to bed, snuggled under the covers and stretched my arms over my head and touched the bedhead with my fingers. Suddenly, I felt a searing pain, like being stabbed by a hot needle. I quickly pulled my hand away and tried to look for a wound. Other than a little reddening around my fingertip, there was nothing to see. I got out of bed and went to get some sympathy from my wife.

While she was looking at the swelling finger, I felt it go numb. Then, the numbness spread from one finger to my hand. A few seconds later, it started to spread up my forearm. I felt a little worried about this creeping affliction and was wondering where it would stop. After another minute, my arm was numb all the way to my elbow. After an hour with no further spread, some feeling came back, starting with a slight tingling and a return of a painful finger.

I went into the bedroom to look for the creature that had attacked me, but found nothing. We pulled the bedcovers off, and shook them. Still nothing. I crawled around under the bed with a flashlight. Nothing to be seen. I felt a little anxious about going back to bed with the unknown creature still lurking around somewhere.

It might bite something more important than a finger next time!

If anyone knows what sort of nasty can do that. Please let me know.

Sometimes the Greek language can be really confusing.

I was sitting on our patio in the garden, stabbing at my keyboard. Luckily, my last book seems to be doing OK in the rankings, so I was keen to get another effort to the editor in the hope of another publication.

For years I have been struggling to speak Greek, and am still finding it really hard. I seemed to be mastering the art when we spent time in Glyfada near Athens, but since we built our home on the island of Evia, my education had to begin all over again. I had been learning Athenian Greek and certainly was not ready for the regional accents and dialects of the Greek islands. I sat and listened to conversations and felt I've learned nothing from my years in Greece. I struggled to understand the most basic phrases.

I had experienced this as a kid. My grandfather was from Tyneside and a broad Geordie.

"A ye gannen the match?" (are you going to the football match?)

"Gan canny or we'll dunsh summick." (Please drive carefully).

I didn't understand a word until I was twelve years old, and even then, struggled to understand most of the discussion.

But, living on a Greek island, I had to learn their accents. So, Alex gave me a shopping list, and I went to the local market.

Top of the list was bread. I had already suffered with this one. When I first started to learn Greek, she sent me to the baker's to ask for *psoli*. I should have asked for *psomi*, but Alex always loved to embarrass me.

Next on the list was *barbounia*, then *fassolia*. I had a feeling that *barbounia* was a type of fish, and *fassolia* was a bean, but wasn't sure. I wandered around the market, found a chap selling beans and asked him for *barbounia*. He smiled and pointed to the fish guy across the way. I got some beans from him and went over and got a kilo of fish.

Alex smiled as she examined my shopping bag.

"Why did you buy the fish?" she asked.

"It's on the list," I replied.

She explained that *barbounia fassolia* was not a fish, it's a type of bean.

"So why call it a fish?"

"It's a special bean the colour of a fish."

It's only in Athens that *barbounia* is a bean. Here it's a fish. Still confused, I went back to writing while Alex cooked the fish.

I might go fishing tomorrow. Alex still needs beans.

Tomatoes only taste good in Greece.

Throughout history and from the dawn of civilisation, the Greeks have been leaders in invention and innovation. Greece, the birthplace of democracy, the home of philosophy, and world leaders in invention.

The ancient Greeks pioneered the use of water mills, inventing both the water wheel itself and the toothed gearing to turn it.

Born in 460 BC, we regard Hippocrates as the "Father of Modern Medicine". He was the first person to reject the notion that illnesses were punishments inflicted by the gods or the result of other such superstitions.

But, the most incredible Greek invention was when someone discovered the art of the

Greek salad. The gods themselves have handed the marriage of tomatoes, feta and olive oil down from Olympus. Over the centuries, this has become Greece.

Tomatoes are a strange fruit. They taste so different depending on where you eat them.

In history, they regarded tomatoes with suspicion as botanists recognised them as a nightshade, a relative of the poisonous belladonna. The interaction of the tomato's acidic juice confirmed this with pewter plates.

The original wild tomatoes were from South America and were the size of peas. Aztecs would mix them up with chilli and bird excrement to make a sauce. I can imagine the ancient Aztec wife asking her husband,

"What would you like for dinner tonight?"

"How about bird droppings and some of those little red peas?" he replies.

I wonder who was the first human to eat bird droppings, and why?

Luckily, the Greeks decided against adding that interesting ingredient to their cuisine and served tomatoes with feta instead.

Greek tomatoes differ from any other I have ever tasted. I often browse the selection in my local supermarket in the UK, looking for something that may taste the same as the incredibly tasty Mediterranean version, but am always disappointed. There is just something special about a good Greek salad made in Greece.

What do you think?

July

IN OUR GREEK VILLAGE

Creating memories of Greece.

If you want to arrive as a tourist, and leave as a tourist, don't come to Greece. If you want to arrive as a tourist and leave as friends, then this is the place for you.

On smaller islands and villages, don't expect perfection. The shower curtain could be missing, the air conditioner may rattle a bit, and you only get hot water when the sun shines. But you will not find the most important reason for going to Greece in a travel brochure.

It's the people who make the difference ...

It was July, and it was hot. Most of the families had gone off to their island, away from the heat of Athens. So, we decided to find an island we had never visited. We had no plans, so just went to the port, and found the first ferry departing and drove on. A few hours later, we arrived in Kalymnos.

We drove past the sponge market and found the tourist office. There we found a brochure for a hotel near Masouri beach. It looked wonderful and had a pool with a view of nearby Telendos. A quick phone call secured our three-day reservation.

We arrived at the hotel determined to spend a few days doing nothing but lounging around the pool, eating and drinking. It would be luxurious.

But there was a problem. The pool was empty and had an enormous crack at the base where the water had leaked out.

Maria, the hotel owner, joined us at the side of the empty pool. Her face was tear-stained as she explained that the pool had cracked a few days ago and she couldn't find anyone to fix it.

"I have to cancel so many bookings," she sobbed.

But unknown to her, this was her lucky day.

"Don't worry. We will fix it," Alex assured her.

It was pure luck. My honest job, while not

writing, was as a waterproofing consultant. I gave her a list of materials I needed. We started work. Alex did most of the digging. I did the repair work. Maria kept us fed with sandwiches and coffee. We really had fun, and after two days of labour, we finished. We let the new concrete set and cure overnight. The next day, we filled it with water.

Maria was delighted. "How much do I owe you?" she asked.

We had had so much fun; we didn't want any money. It was enough to see a smiling Maria and a sparkling pool. But we accepted her offer of a meal at her cousin's *taverna* on the nearby island of Telendos.

That evening, a boat arrived at the beach and whisked us the short distance to the small island. Maria was already there with her family as we joined the family at the table. We were so close to the sea that we could almost dip our toes in the cool water. It was idyllic.

Maria's cousin Tasos came over to the table, gave us a big smile, and thanked us for helping her.

"Anything you want, I will cook," he informed us.

"Do you have any grilled octopus?" I asked.

"One moment," he replied and disappeared into the kitchen.

A minute later, his waiter appeared wearing a swimming costume and a diver's mask, holding a trident. He waded into the sea. We watched him swim in circles until his head popped up, and he held his trident in the air with a wriggling octopus on the forks.

That was the best payment we could ever have expected. There was no way Tasos was going to disappoint us. If we wanted octopus, he would make sure we got it.

The next day, we kissed Maria and packed our bags into the car to depart. Maria came running out with a black bin bag. Inside were four octopuses.

"That's a present from Tasos," she said.

Many years later, we are still friends with this lovely family.

And the pool never leaked again.

Funny Greek car hire.

I arrived at Athens airport. Kostas, the car hire rep, was at Arrivals waving a card with my name on in one hand, the other holding a frappé.

Following him out of the terminal into the car park, he asked me to hold his coffee while he disappeared and returned with my shiny new car. He left the engine running while we checked for any lumps and bumps before giving me his card and assuring me that if there was any problem, I should just call.

I jumped into the driving seat. Alex got into the passenger seat. We waved at Kostas and drove away.

Whenever we arrive at the airport, our first destination is always a fish *taverna* a short distance away by the sea. We took our table, cast our eyes over the sparkling Aegean Sea, looked at each other and smiled. We had arrived home.

After a leisurely meal we left, got into the car, pressed the starter button, and nothing happened. I pressed it again; the car still didn't start. I rummaged around in my pocket, found Kostas's card and called the number. It rang and rang, but there was no answer.

I tried again, still no answer. After the tenth attempt, this was not working. I checked the card for another number, nothing. So, I decided to go to his office and try to find him there. But the address was in central Athens, and I was stuck outside a *taverna* near Glyfada. I needed a taxi. I left Alex to admire the view from the *taverna* and left.

Hailing a Greek taxi is an interesting experience. But to actually get them to take you anywhere takes diplomacy and patience. They will only allow you to get into the car if your destination coincides with theirs.

The first taxi stopped. The driver asked, "Where do you want to go?"

"Central Athens," I replied.

"But I'm not going there," he informed me. "I'm on the way to Castella. Can I take you there?"

Although this was a kind offer and nearer to my destination than my current location, I declined the offer and tried another taxi. The next one stopped with the same result, but he was going to Voula, which is in the opposite direction.

After two more attempts and with me still standing beside the road with my aching arm in the air, one stopped. After considering my request, he begrudgingly allowed me into the back seat.

I think he resented having me in his taxi and took his revenge by scaring me half to death with the speed of his driving, weaving around cars, lorries and kissing the bumper of a police car before accelerating down a side street claiming it to be a shortcut while keeping his eyes in the mirror in case we were being chased. Being in this cab reminded me of the one and only time I went on a roller coaster, and then I was vomiting for a week afterwards.

But we arrived fast.

I jumped out of the taxi at my destination, feeling wobbly and a little sick. I entered the office and asked for Kostas.

"He's in the cafe along the road," the receptionist informed me.

So off I went in search of the cafe. I finally

found him, sitting in a group sucking his frappé from a straw.

Recognition spread across his face as I approached.

"How's the car?" he asked.

"Answer your bloody phone," I replied.

He fished around in his pocket and found his mobile and scrolled down his missed calls.

"Oh sorry, it was on silent."

I explained that he had given me a defective car, and I was most upset. He looked at me.

"But it's almost new," he said.

"But the bloody thing won't start!"

"Tell me what happened," he said.

I told him we came out of the *taverna* after a lovely meal, pressed the start button, and nothing happened. The bloody car wouldn't start and must be broken.

"You know it's a hybrid, don't you?" he asked.

"Wassat?" I replied.

He looked at me like a parent trying to explain to a particularly stupid child.

"It's electric most of the time," he said. "You won't hear it. Just put it in gear and drive away. The engine will cut in automatically."

The only other experience I had previously

had with an electric vehicle was when I borrowed the local milkman's float when I was ten.

For all those other dinosaurs out there, be warned. Sometimes when you start a car, you can't hear the engine. You could avoid a ride in a Greek taxi and save your life.

Are you a thinker?

Sorry folks. My mood is a little more serious today. Don't worry. I will be back tomorrow with more funny stories from my Greek village. But I must get this off my chest.

When was the last time you had an opinion? Was that opinion formed from your own experience, or was it based on someone else's, which you conveniently adopted?

In these days of worldwide twenty-four-hour news broadcasts and ready access to social media, we have become lazy and stopped thinking. Opinions are based upon viral stories and news articles propagated by anyone with a vested interest and shared with the masses. Not what we actually see with our own eyes or experience ourselves. But we must get our opinions from somewhere. At least we don't need to think about it. It's oven-ready and packaged for consumption. So rather than look for the truth, we share it with others, which then also becomes their opinion.

We in the Western world feel that we don't need to dig any deeper than the surface. Our politicians, through tame media outlets, tell us what to think. And most of us accept it. On the other side comes social media. A quick browse through Google will assure you that the earth is flat, the British royal family are lizards, and little green men live happily in our town. This leaves us confused and vulnerable.

Rogue states have enormous propaganda machines to spread disinformation, which is rapidly shared with the world, gathering credibility at every stage. But you don't need to look too far. Other countries do the same. Look at Brexit.

We jump from one opinion to another until we finally settle for the majority and stick with that. Once that opinion is formed, it slowly becomes a belief. A belief is worth fighting for. How many people have suffered and died for a belief? It's our most powerful human instinct. And where did it come from?

Greeks ask questions. Greece is the cradle of civilisation and home to philosophy. Greeks have rarely enjoyed stability. They view a government of whatever colour with suspicion and have learned to question it. I have heard it said that Greeks are more inclined to adopt conspiracy theories. This is not the case. They will just not accept information spoon-fed to them. No, they want to be convinced, discuss every angle and arrive at their own opinion. Sometimes, this means looking closely at an unpopular subject or questioning an underlying reason. The conversation is heated and unpleasant. There are no taboo subjects, just open and frank, and sometimes violent discussions from every angle before they reach an agreement.

As a Brit, I never learned to question. People above me would always do what was best for me. I never doubted that. This lulled me into a warm bath of ignorance.

Living with a Greek wife has changed that way of thinking. It didn't happen overnight. I needed to be shocked out of my stupor and open my eyes to the world. A little like having a rotten tooth removed, it hurts like hell at first, but you are eventually pleased it happened.

In Ukraine, genocide is happening now. Innocent people are dying. The Russian people are bystanders suffering the result of one man's power-hungry aspirations. The actual news has been cut off; the propaganda machine has done its job.

But slowly, they are turning their backs on the official line and forming their own opinions. Once this is over, and we examine the carcass of this war, can anyone say we are blameless? If we survive this, we need to ensure it never happens again.

Are all Greek women so fit?

I think I am still married, but I rarely see my wife. I leave for work long before she wakes in the morning and usually arrive home hearing pounding beats radiating into the street and my front door shaking so much that the keyhole is a blur.

No, it's not an illicit love affair, nor is she holding part-time rave parties. She is a Zumba fanatic.

She usually does two to three hours every day except Sundays. Plus, every evening there are another two sessions either by Zoom, or at her local health club. So, that's a minimum of twenty hours per week.

If it's via Zoom, I disappear into my bedroom with our dogs to avoid being kicked to death. The dogs always know what's coming and escape first. We sit there with the house shaking, the rumble of Latino music pounding our ears while waiting for the session to end so I can pop around the village to apologise to the neighbours.

I have suggested a different hobby more in keeping with her age. Maybe bomb disposal. At least that would be quieter (most of the time).

Luckily, we do manage to get some respite during nighttime hours, but I did catch her looking at other Zoom-based Zumba sessions in different time zones. Surely she must need to sleep sometime?

But it makes her happy, so that makes me happy.

The art of canoeing in Greece

Act your age, Peter! You are not a teenager any more. Old people should not play with boats.

I had the great idea of buying two inflatable canoes. Visions of Alex and I happily paddling up and down the beach, stopping for a coffee in one of the seaside cafes and passing a few hours getting fitter. I even thought of paddling over to Skiathos once we had become a little more proficient.

So, we pulled the boats out of the car, and set about pumping them up and putting the plugs in the right holes. There they were: two new, impressive-looking canoes sitting on the beach, waiting for our adventure.

We waded into the sea, towing the boats

behind us. We thought of a quick trip to the little church on the nearby island and a leisurely paddle around the bay. Alex threw her leg over hers and smoothly dropped into the seat and paddled away. I lifted one leg. A puff of wind sent the canoe towards me. I fell backwards with the boat on top of me and drowned my new hat as I somersaulted under the water.

I tried again. This time, I checked the wind direction and turned it downwind. I lifted one leg into it. The wind puffed again, and the canoe left to sail away with my leg still stuck inside it. After being dragged a few metres with my hat acting as a parachute, we finally stopped, and I managed to free my leg.

This was not going well. I looked up. Alex was a spot in the distance and had almost reached the church on the island. I was still trying to get on my uncooperative boat. I tried again. I put the boat into the wind. Threw a leg over. Tried to lift the other one. The boat turned over and threw me off, and floated away, leaving me blowing water out of my nose.

I tried again. This time, I used my legs to launch myself belly first onto the boat. My thinking was that perhaps if I could lie on it, I could sort my legs out later. This didn't work. I was just lying on the thing, scared to move in any direction as the slightest change in weight resulted in me sitting on the seabed with the boat over my head.

By this time, Alex was on her way back. I could hear the giggles as she approached. I gave up the idea of sitting in the thing. The hole in the middle had obviously been designed for children, so I decided the best way to paddle a canoe was lying on top with my belly squeezing through the hole and the paddle above my head.

I couldn't really concentrate as I was distracted by Alex's giggling and the howls of laughter from people sitting on the beach watching the show.

I've given up canoeing now. I need a bigger boat.

The philosophy of Alex.

Culture and religion in Greece go hand in hand. You cannot have one without the other. This is true of most ancient civilisations, but especially in Greece. We are reminded of the part religion has always played in Greece by the thousands of shrines dedicated to the ancient gods scattered throughout the country and islands. Then, in 49 AD, St Paul arrived, and things began to change.

My wife, Alex, is a modern, progressive ball of fire. She can turn the air blue when upset, and is not slow to give an opinion when it matters. She is keen to adopt new ways. She is open-minded and a deep thinker. The genes of ancient philosophers run in her blood and her enquiring mind will question any subject presented to her using her famous Greek logic.

Being a writer, I sometimes wander into fantasy. But not for long. Alex will listen to my opinion, then sweetly pick away at the threads of my argument until all I have left is a threadbare, disproved theory and a feeling of embarrassment for being so stupid.

But as with most Greeks, religion rules.

In our homes in Greece and England, we have a corner of a room dedicated to religion. An oil burner, candles, and a few photos of family members under the protection of an icon propped up against the wall.

Early in our relationship. Alex took me to Tinos to visit the icon. We stepped off the ferry and walked to the base of a hill. At the top of the long straight road was the church of Panagia Evangelistria. There was a thin strip of red carpet running up the side of the road. As we climbed the hill, we stopped to buy a few candles before continuing our climb.

As we approached the courtyard of the church, I turned to speak to Alex. She wasn't there. I looked down, and there she was, crawling on her hands and knees. Her short skirt had been replaced by a long grey dress which covered her arms, body and legs, and on her head was a grey scarf. I stood back and followed behind as she crawled up the marble staircase and into the church. I found her kneeling in front of the icon, tears in her eyes, and hands pressed together.

This is a culture to be proud of. It doesn't matter if you are Christian, Muslim, Jew or atheist. Greeks don't judge.

Philoxenia applies to all.

I caught Covid

Three weeks ago, I had a little plastic test kit with two red lines showing. It wasn't the full-blooded life-hanging-by-a-thread version; more the unleaded, Covid-light, sugar-free sniffle version. I think it's because I've had three vaccinations, so I'm told I should be fairly safe.

But I didn't tell my wife that. She owed me sympathy, and lots of it.

Over the years, like most men, I've suffered with bouts of man flu. Men will know only too well that this is a nasty and serious disease. We try to explain why we feel too ill to help around the house. We find it difficult to get out of our comfy chair in front of the TV, and even find it difficult walking to the fridge for another beer.

We plead with our wives and girlfriends for some sort of understanding and, if not too much trouble, a little sympathy. But it falls on deaf ears. This time I had proof of my illness. Did it make any difference? Of course not. She still expected me to take the bins out, walk the dogs, and lift my legs while she vacuumed the carpet. She also forced me to wear a mask around the house in case I gave my disease to the dogs.

"All men are babies," they tell us. "You should try childbirth," we are informed.

They ignore our suffering and pass off our serious affliction as "only a cold".

Perhaps modern technology will invent a test for man flu in the future. That will show them.

Three weeks later, my wife hadn't caught it. Her vaccinations worked. They had given me a defective batch. But at least I have passed Covid. That's over and done with. Until the next time.

Just to get the blood pumping.
A LITTLE SNIPPET FROM MY BOOK

We sipped our coffee and gazed at the Acropolis with the majestic Parthenon sitting proudly atop it, towering over the city in the warm Greek sunshine.

I wondered if by constructing our very own replica Parthenon on the roof of our new apartment block we might compensate in some tiny way for the fact that the real structure had lost some of its treasures to London's British Museum. Might it be taken as one Englishman's apology for his countryman's abuse of Greek hospitality?

This is a sore subject for Greeks, who claim that Lord Elgin stole pieces of their revered monuments during his service as ambassador to the court of the Ottoman sultan. The British say that they were purchased; the Greeks prefer to use the term looted. Between 1801 and 1812, Lord Elgin snaffled half the surviving marbles and spirited them out of Greece. The British Government insists he bought them from their legal owners. The problem is that the legal owners at the time were the occupying Turks.

During our last trip to England, Alex wanted to visit the British Museum, saying she wanted to see the Tutankhamun exhibition. I was also keen to see it and innocently agreed to accompany her.

As we entered the museum, we were confronted with an enormous sign that read:

ELGIN MARBLES: THIS WAY

A large arrow pointing to the left. Alex pulled me towards it. I pulled back, in the direction of the Egyptian hall. I then realised that she had duped me. Alex had no interest in dead pharaohs. She was there to reclaim her stolen property.

We stepped into the hall and onto the white marble floor. There ahead of us were the beautiful relics. An ornately carved frieze stretched the length of an entire wall. The sculpture known as the "Horse of Selene" had pride of place, together with an abundance of precious artefacts under careful lighting designed to show them in their full glory.

My eye was immediately drawn to a carving of a bearded centaur holding a young man by the throat. The poor man had lost his penis, which seemed to have been snapped off.

By the look on Alex's face, I was likely to be the next person to suffer that indignation. She was not impressed. She turned to me and said,

"You are a fxxxxxx pirate."

I was shocked. She'd never sworn at me in English before, and she obviously thought I was somehow personally responsible for the theft of her heritage. I tried to comfort her by pointing out how well-cared for the sculptures were, mumbling something about the nice presentation.

But she was getting angrier. Alex has a temper, though thankfully it rarely burns hot for long. Concerned that she would make a fuss in the middle of the hall, I searched for ways to defuse it. I settled on an attack strategy. I took her arm and looked into her eyes.

"How dare you swear at me?" I said. "And I'm not a pirate either."

This seemed to work. She had, in her anger misdirected her rage towards me and was now feeling sorry about that.

So before her fury reignited, I led her out of the hall, suggesting we look at something else. We walked around some other areas of the museum, but she was uninterested in the displays.

"So which part of this massive museum houses the British exhibits?" she asked sarcastically.

I fumbled to answer that question. Obviously, the Egyptian relics were not British, nor were the Parthenon Marbles.

After peeking into hall after hall, I did eventually find a small section on ancient Britain, but this was dwarfed by the huge displays from China, Africa and the Americas. I realised I was not going to win this one. I had suddenly become personally responsible for my country's avarice and its looting of the world for treasures that were now sitting in glass cases staring accusingly at me.

As we sat outside the modest pavement cafe in Athens, relishing what had to be one of the best views in the world, I felt both privileged and a little guilty. I did feel sorry for Alex. As a true-blooded Greek, she could not simply look at this wonder of the world and appreciate the beauty and magnificence of this incredible piece of history; as she gazed at it, all she could think about was that her heritage had been stolen away and was currently residing in a far-away country that had claimed Greece's precious artefacts as its own.

Although, I did build a new Parthenon on our roof in nearby Glyfada, especially for Alex.

But perhaps it's not quite the same.

August
IN OUR GREEK VILLAGE

Decorating the garden.

Today, Alex decided to paint the trees in our garden. She had seen some trees in the village with white trunks and thought they looked nice. I was more than happy with the current colour of our trees, but Alex did her usual trick of nodding at me as I explained I thought they look nice as they are, and painted them anyway.

First, she took me to the local hardware shop. She asked the owner for twenty litres of white paint.

"Do you want to paint walls inside or outside?" he asked.

"Outside. But not walls, trees," she informed him.

He laughed and told her it was not paint

she needed but a special paste which we could buy from the builders' merchant.

So, we got some. Alex is at this moment painting our trees.

She has already asked me if I think our lawn would look better blue.

Adjusting your bits

The national pastime of fine-tuning and adjustment of private parts is a necessary fact of modern life for men worldwide. Since the invention of trousers, men have struggled to encapsulate their bits in the most comfortable way, but without success.

We sit on a chair; the parts have somehow moved from a comfortable position at the front of our bodies and migrated underneath, allowing one bottom cheek to squish one of our three important pieces, causing pain and discomfort. We then need to surreptitiously drop something on the floor in a pretext to picking up the fallen item. While bending over, we can quickly sort things out and reposition the errant straggler, and hope nobody noticed. We constantly battle with our very own flaw of nature, wondering why God left our favourite bits unprotected and free to wander, getting themselves into trouble and trapped between chairs and bottom cheeks, when our brain was given a protective shell and obediently stays where God put it.

This is the fate of man. But in Greece there is an additional and much more serious reason for protecting your stuff.

Alex and I were walking along the road, and a priest was coming towards us.

"Quick, grab your balls," she told me.

I was confused. Why would the presence of a priest necessitate grabbing my private parts? But I complied. As the priest passed, he smiled knowingly.

This seemed a strange command. But the convention is that you should turn and run away, holding your testicles. This harks back to when Christianity took hold of the ancient Greek world. There was widespread destruction of Hellenic nude statues, especially their genitals; the early Christians took hammers and broke off the penis and testicles from every sculpture. After that, whenever ethnic Greeks saw a priest coming, they would tell each other to hold on to their balls.

When Alex and I were on the island of Tinos, making our pilgrimage to the hilltop church of Panagia Evangelistria, there were so many priests around that my hand never left my crotch during the entire visit.

We greet priests all over the world in so many ways. But none so strangely as in Greece.

Catching pneumonia...in August.

I was feeling poorly. It was August and the temperature, as usual, was nudging forty degrees, but unfortunately so was mine. I finally stopped fighting Alex and agreed to go to the local clinic.

After a quick X-ray, they wheeled me in to see the results. Three doctors were studying my X-ray. There was a picture of my chest on the screen. One lung looked nice and white, the other in contrast was mostly black. The doctors were mumbling and drawing air over their teeth, a little like a car mechanic giving you the bad news about your suspect big ends.

One doctor turned to me, and with a sad look on his face, said, "Go to the cancer hospital in Athens immediately."

I didn't like where this was going. But had no choice. By the time the taxi arrived in Athens, I had written my will, checked my life insurance and resigned myself to my imminent eternal rest.

We walked in and were met by a lovely doctor. She checked my temperature, which was forty-one degrees, looked at the X-ray and announced her diagnosis.

"You have pneumonia."

I was delighted. Alex smiled at the doctor, who assured her I would need to be admitted for a few days, but I should be OK.

The ward contained four beds. Next to me, there was a chap with his hands and feet bound by bandages to the bed rails.

Opposite, a sad-looking man stared at me and announced he was here because he couldn't fart.

On the other side was a poorly looking man with tubes in his mouth connected to a brown machine under the bed which looked like a set of bellows which emitted regular breathing sounds.

The doctors and nurses fussed around me, inserted drips into my arm and gave me a cocktail of tablets, then left. I sent Alex home and tried to sleep.

A few moments later, the guy tied to the bed next to me managed to free one arm and got himself tangled up in a bandage which wrapped itself around his throat. He started to look blue. I called out to the nurse.

"Yes?" came a voice from an intercom above the door.

"I think the guy tied to the bed is having trouble," I shouted into the box.

"And I still can't fart," added the man opposite.

A few moments later, a nurse arrived, unwound the bandages from his neck, and retied the poor man. She ignored the man who couldn't fart and turned to leave.

"Why is he tied up?" I asked.

"Because he keeps trying to climb out of the window," she shrugged.

"Is the guy with tubes OK?" I asked. "He looks a little grey."

"Oh, I think he's dead, but the family won't agree to turn off the machine," she replied.

The nurse had been gone for only two minutes when the bandaged man freed a leg and started to kick the wall with such force that his foot bled.

I called up at the box.

"Nurse?"

"Yes?"

"The bandaged man has freed his leg and is kicking the wall. He's bleeding now," I yelled.

"I still can't fart," added the man opposite.

She arrived to retie the bandaged man while swearing under her breath and left again.

I was still feeling poorly and fell asleep. I woke to a smell of burning. The box connected to the guy with tubes was smoking and making strange grinding noises. The guy next to me had managed to unravel his bandages and there was a pungent smell in the air mixing with the smoke.

"Nurse?"

"What now?"

"The dead guy is on fire. The guy tied to the bed has just jumped out of the window, and the guy that couldn't fart, now can …"

Alex with a chainsaw.

As we live in Greece, the birthplace of democracy, my wife and I discuss everything. Alex asks my opinion, I give it, we come to an agreement which she then ignores and does what she wants anyway.

We are waiting for friends to arrive to stay with us for a while. Alex is busy getting the house ready and fine-tuning the garden. She has already painted the tree trunks white, along with herself. She finished with the trees, and still had some paint left, so was prowling the garden looking for something else that may look nice painted white. She managed to apply a few brush strokes to my traditional bread oven. I spend an hour with a scrubbing brush and hosepipe dealing with that.

If Alex with a paintbrush is dangerous, imagine my concern when she asked for a chainsaw...

"Sorry, but I will not buy you a chainsaw," I told her. "I like the trees as they are, and you would probably chop your legs off."

So, this morning I woke up to a loud buzzing sound. Because I refused to buy her a chainsaw, she went off and found someone that owned one, and through sleepy eyes, I looked out of my bedroom window at the devastation.

There was Alex, standing under a tree. High in its branches was a man cutting away at my precious trees with a chainsaw. Branches strewn all over the garden.

Never mind. I'm sure they will grow again... eventually. At least I can wave at the neighbours now.

I love living here.

Tasteful Greek garden design.

"I want a flamingo," Alex informed me.
"What, a real one?" I asked.
"No. one of those."

I followed her pointing finger towards a roadside shop selling plants and garden furniture. There was a selection of brightly-painted fibreglass animals and birds, all lined up in a row.

At the end was a strange-looking bird with a curved beak and evil eyes watching me. Its feathers were painted the colour of school dinner blancmange. It was horrible.

We had spent the last two weeks working on our garden, and apart from Alex painting the trees, then trying to use the leftover paint to change the colour of my ornate brick-built

BBQ, then bringing a lumberjack with a chainsaw to devastate my prized pine trees, I thought I had got away lightly.

The lawn was nicely trimmed, and trees were pruned. The garden was looking good. A plastic pink flamingo in the middle of the lawn was the last thing my Greek garden needed. But Alex had other ideas.

We arrived home. I opened the boot of the car. There, staring at me, was not one, but two ugly pink birds. I had just crossed the road for two minutes to buy some water from the kiosk. In those few moments, she had bought the birds and stuffed them into the boot of the car without a word.

The garden still looks pretty, but now with yellow-eyed pink birds watching my every move.

I'm sure I'll get used to them, eventually. I might buy a garden gnome to keep them company.

Alex strikes again.

It's so peaceful in my Greek village garden. No buzzing of chainsaws, no bulldozers assaulting my garden. The only sound is the crickets in the trees and the light breeze ruffling the tree branches.

Why is it so peaceful? Alex hasn't woken up yet. She is still asleep lying in bed with green hair and knees. I did wonder why my wife had changed her hair colour. I quite liked it the way it used to be. Perhaps she wanted to dye her hair to match the garden?

No, on further investigation, I found out the reason. I walked onto the lawn. It was sticky. I looked down. My feet were green. I looked up and saw my nice previously snow-white wall had turned the same colour as my feet.

I had enjoyed a glass of *ouzo* last night after watching a great concert in the village and went to bed. While I was sleeping, Alex sprang into action to continue her quest to change the colour of my garden and painted the walls green.

I wish she had painted those evil-eyed flamingos too.

Greek ferry trip. (Part 1)

Back in the UK now after an incredible drive through Europe. What a trip!

The first leg of our journey from Greece was to take the ferry from Patra to Ancona. We have done this trip several times so had an idea of what to expect.

As we entered the port, we drove through customs. A large man with a clipboard smoking a cigarette waved us straight through. In the other lane, a car had been stopped and open suitcases were lying on the floor with clothes and possessions spread over the tarmac. We obviously didn't look dodgy. Alex was distracted playing with her phone and had a rare innocent look on her face...

We drove up the ramp and into the ship and were directed down a steep ramp below the waterline. There was a parking attendant shouting at everyone and trying to squeeze us into spaces half the width of the car. We would have trouble getting a bicycle into the offered space but followed his directions.

"Park there. No, not there, *there*. No, you idiot, do it again!"

He was finally content when we managed to park so close to the metal hull that there was not enough space to pass a cigarette paper.

Another car was directed to park next to ours, so close we had to fold in our wing mirrors. We couldn't open the doors, so we climbed out of the window. This was our first taste of *Fawlty Towers* at sea.

We grabbed our overnight bags and climbed the stairs to find our cabin. As we ended the long corridor to our room, an old man in a ship's uniform jumped out.

"Go away!" he shouted.

I waved our room pass at him and assured him we had a cabin.

"Go away," he repeated. "Room not ready."

We were tired and hungry so decided to go

to the restaurant to wait for our cabin to be ready. It was closed. Tables were set, fine tablecloths were laid out with wine glasses upturned but there were no staff. I found a passing officer and asked him when it was due to open.

"Perhaps it will open soon, but perhaps not," he informed us and wandered away.

Still none the wiser we sat and waited. Finally, the staff arrived and let us in. We walked into the empty restaurant area and went to sit down.

"Not there, sit there!" he demanded and squeezed us into a small corner.

He had been taking lessons from the parking guy downstairs. I was sitting on a bench with my shoulder touching the wall, and Alex was pressed in beside me.

Soon, other tables started to fill with other people barred from their cabins. The food was good, and we enjoyed our meal.

The family at the next table got up and left, and the waiter came to clear their table.

"Pigs!" he yelled. "Look at the state of that table!" he pointed at the mess and looked at us. "Next time they come here I will throw their food on the floor; they can eat from there. If they want to act like animals, I will treat them as animals."

MUSINGS FROM A GREEK VILLAGE

We quickly rearranged our table to make it as neat as possible before he came back to clean ours.

Greek ferry trip. (Part 2)

Finally, we could go to our cabin. It was beautifully comfortable. There were two windows overlooking the bow and we could watch as we left the port heading for the open sea. There was a fridge holding some water and fruit, a large armchair and a small settee near the windows and a double bed.

On the table was a paper cordially inviting us to attend the *à la carte* restaurant for a complimentary breakfast in the morning. We were fairly sure we left our table clean on our last visit, so we hoped we would not be eating our breakfast off the floor.

As the ship sailed towards Corfu, we got into bed and relaxed with the humming of the engines and were rocked to sleep by the gentle swaying of the ship.

Early the next morning, Alex shook me awake and threw a lifejacket on the bed. There she was, standing wearing hers already and demanding I put mine on too. She had seen some dark clouds out of the window, and the rain was splashing onto the glass. The ship was still gently rocking. I had heard no alarms.

"Can we have breakfast before we abandon ship?" I asked.

She looked out of the window and was reassured to see the water was still calm and agreed.

"I want to keep my life jacket on though," she insisted.

I suggested that the sight of her walking through the ship wearing a lifejacket was probably not a good idea as it may cause panic and frighten the captain, so she reluctantly agreed to take it off.

They served our breakfast on a table, not the floor so we must have made a good impression with yesterday's meal. The waiter was still miserable and complaining, but reluctantly poured our coffee while muttering through his mask when a guy with a big black beard wandered in and sat down.

"What are you doing here?" he yelled at the chap. "You're a truck driver. You shouldn't be in this restaurant. You should be in the self-service restaurant with your own kind."

"But it's busy in there. I just want to have a quiet breakfast. Look I can pay." He held out a small wad of cash to prove it.

"Okay. You can stay. But keep your elbows off the table and eat properly."

Back in our cabin, we spent the day relaxing and reading. We had no Wi-Fi on board, but my phone was picking up navigation, so I could see where we were. Still on open sea and around 2 hours from our destination, there came a knock at the door.

"Get out now, we need to clean the cabin."

"But we are at least two hours from port," I protested.

"Doesn't matter. Get out now and go to the lounge," he insisted.

So, we dragged our suitcases to the lounge. It was still full of people with their camp beds, makeshift tents, and pillows scattered over the floor.

The already crowded deck was becoming more crowded as passengers were fast being evicted from their cabins. So we huddled there with the rest until we finally arrived at port and the stampede began to get to our cars.

We followed the crowds down the winding staircase to the lower garage level. It was hot down there. Sweat was dripping into my eyes as I watched people climbing over parked vehicles because there was no space to walk between them, all with their bags held in their teeth.

Then the engines began to start. Drivers who had made it to their vehicles were hot and needed to start their air conditioning and were revving their engines, not considering the possibility that the rest of us would expire from carbon monoxide poisoning.

We didn't fancy the climb, so we just waited by the door for cars to move while feeling lightheaded and with fast-warming car engines adding to the heat.

What a great trip! I will certainly book again soon. When more material is needed for my next book.

Driving through France.

I am having such a lovely time in Reims. We are trying to order in a restaurant and failing.

Alex is great at language. Greek being her mother tongue, she speaks perfect English, Spanish and Italian, with some Portuguese.

But no French.

I watched her squabble with the waiter, and mentioned it was nice to see she also struggled with the language.

"I'm not struggling," she informed me. "He is."

Meet Bella, our Anglo-Greek dog.

Bella, like me, was born in England. If I was going to start a new life in Greece, then Bella, as part of the family, would join us.

Two problems. First, we had to get her here. The only practical way would be the long drive through Europe and a ferry from Venice.

Second, she had just entered the dreaded puppy chewing phase and had developed a passion for chair legs and door frames.

Our route would take us through France, Switzerland, and into Italy to catch the ferry to Patra leaving from Venice. We should be able to get to Venice with only two overnight stops before a thirty-six-hour ferry trip, so we studied Google for dog-friendly hotels along our route.

Stop One: Chateau Hotel, Champagne, France.

We drove into the car park outside the imposing medieval castle. There was a drawbridge over the moat leading to the reception. As I opened the car door and let Bella out, she spotted the moat. Before I had a chance to clip on her lead, she was off. After two laps around the castle, she finally heard my yells, left the water, and came bounding back. The hotel staff refused to let her in until she had fully dried, and the mud was washed off.

I awoke in the middle of the night to hear a crunching sound. She was busy eating the leg of an antique table. After settling the bill and making a large contribution towards the repair of the antique furniture, we were politely asked not to return.

We set off towards Italy.

Stop Two: Lake Como, Italy.

We stopped outside the imposing hotel on the shore of Lake Como. This time, we made sure we fully secured Bella before letting her out of the car. The hotel was lovely, and they had made a bed for the dogs in our room. She looked sleepy after the long drive, so we felt fairly safe leaving her in the room while we went to have dinner in the restaurant.

When we returned, the room was wrecked. Bedclothes were spread across the floor, and the sheets had been eaten. We cleaned the room and hid the tattered sheets in our suitcase. Perhaps they wouldn't notice?

They did... I received a message that the hotel was going to charge my card for the stolen sheets, then added, *You are no longer welcome at this hotel.*

Stop Three: Ferry from Venice to Patras

I was happy to be on the ferry, and keen to reach Greece with no further trouble. Luckily, the ferry had kennels. At least we could relax and enjoy our cruise through the Adriatic while the dogs were securely confined.

We took Bella to the kennels on the top deck. It was just a row of cages. But the ship needed to be protected from this little eating machine, so we locked her in and went down to the restaurant. I sat and watched Venice pass by as we left port. Alex left me to explore the ship.

When we returned to our cabin. There was Bella with her tail wagging, sitting in the middle of a war zone. Alex's "exploration" of the ship included taking Bella out of the unpleasant kennels and sneaking her into our cabin.

They banned us from every hotel in Europe. Now we were facing a ban from the sea, too. All because of our little Greek dog.

But she was worth the trouble and now lives happily with the rest of our extended animal family.

A fine dining experience. What, no souvlaki?

I am not a disciplined writer. I'm trying to finish the sequel to *A Parthenon on Our Roof*, but my brain keeps getting in the way. Alex is sitting next door giggling at some Facebook posts, and occasionally pops in to read something that she enjoyed.

"So, what's for lunch?" she yells.

We have a deal in our house. I cook on weekends. I love cooking and find it relaxing. Alex's taste in food is fortunately simple. She would be equally happy with a piece of feta cheese and a chunk of bread, rather than a full three-course meal, so no pressure. I just cook what inspires me.

Alex hates fancy food. She also hates food snobbery. She is happy with anything barbecued, cheese pastries, lambs' heads and traditional Greek food. But nothing too exotic.

We recently travelled to and from Greece by car. It was a fantastic journey, and I had pre-booked the hotels along our route. Our first stop was a large French chateau hotel set in the middle of the Champagne region of France.

We went into the dining room for dinner. Bottles of champagne were spread around every wall on shelves and tables, and some were just scattered randomly in corners. In the centre of the room was a huge cut barrel the size of a wagon wheel full of ice with hundreds of bottles of champagne keeping cool.

There were just two choices on the menu. Pigeon in blood, or fish with foam. Alex wrinkled her nose as she studied the menu. She definitely wanted nothing soaked in blood, so reluctantly ordered the fish in foam.

A wine waiter appeared with a silver cup hanging on a silver chain around his neck and gave us the wine list. It was huge, about the size of a family Bible.

Alex thumbed through a few pages, looked up, and asked, "Have you got any champagne?"

The previously talkative waiter was struck dumb as he digested this question and wondered how to respond. He just looked blank as he waved his arms in an arc around the room, pointing at the thousands of bottles on display.

Alex continued to look at the wine list.

"How about *retsina*?" she asked.

He took the Bible back and searched through the thousands of pages.

"No Madam. We do not have *retsina*."

"OK, I'll have a coke."

I can't take her anywhere.

At last! Home in our village.

It's so good to be back in the village. We have been in the UK for the book launch, but now are back home to paradise.

As we slowly merged back into village culture, I took a walk around my garden. The locals all think us a little strange because we grow things we can't eat. Flowers, ornamental trees and a lawn. The lovely local lady who takes care of our home is determined to educate us on village life. So, during our last absence, she decided to use all of the space in our flower pots to plant vegetables. We now have strange mixes of roses with cucumbers and peppers. Tomatoes are growing alongside carnations. The base of every tree has aubergines sprouting from the ground.

MUSINGS FROM A GREEK VILLAGE

Consider me educated.
I love living here.

Relax. You're in Greece.

This place does things to people. Greece transports you to a different state of mind. The stress of modern living is left behind as we adapt to a different and so much more relaxed life.

We have family staying with us in beautiful Pefki. My Greek brother-in-law lives in Holland with his Dutch wife. My nephew, Darwin, was born in Holland and has adapted to the efficiency of Dutch living. But when he arrived in Greece, his Greek side surfaced. The family spend their sunny days here lounging on the beach, eating at beautiful seaside restaurants. Life has slowed down.

Yesterday, Darwin went shopping with his pretty Dutch girlfriend. He stopped at a petrol station to fill up, but his credit card didn't work when trying to pay for the fuel. They didn't have enough cash, so he left his girlfriend at the petrol station as security while he came home to get some money.

On the way home, he passed Pefki beach, saw a friend and decided to join him for a "quick" coffee. An hour or so later, he arrived home and went to have a shower. He came out of the bathroom wrapped in a towel.

"Hi Darwin," I said, "where's Britt?"

A look of realisation spread over his face as he remembered leaving her at the petrol station. We all jumped into the car to rescue her.

We arrived and found her sitting under a canopy beside the forecourt at a long table eating lunch with the owner's family, a forkful of stuffed tomatoes in one hand and a glass of local wine in the other. As we approached, the family set a few more chairs around the table and invited us to join them for lunch.

Britt forgave Darwin, and we had a lovely lunch with our new friends. This will certainly be included in my new book.

I love living here.

Cool and sexy.

Today we went to the beach. Alex's cousin Bia has come to visit. The sea looked so inviting; she wanted to swim a little. Normally, if Alex and I swim, we pop down to the deserted beach at the end of our road, have a quick dip and come home.

Because Bia was with us, Alex took her to the beach in the village. There were sun loungers, nice straw parasols for shade, and waiter service for drinks. It was quite luxurious.

We put our towels on the sun beds, and we went into the sea. There must have been a storm out to sea, because the waves were enormous. As the beach is pebbly at the shoreline, and me being a wimp, I wore my flip-flops to enter the water.

I splashed around for a few minutes, rode the enormous waves and cooled off. From the sea, I saw the waiter bringing the drinks to our sun beds, so I headed towards the beach to pay. Our spot on the beach was about four rows back from the water. The front few rows were filled with young, tanned, attractive women stretched out in revealing bikinis, watching me as I came towards the beach.

I was doing my James Bond impression, strutting out of the sea, holding my stomach in, when a giant wave came up behind me. I fell forward, face first, somersaulted underwater, with my legs suddenly in the air, and my flip-flops flew off and went in different directions.

As I tried to stand up, another wave hit me from behind. I tumbled over and again tried to stand up again only to find that I was facing the wrong way and was hit in the face by another breaking wave.

So, there I was, lying on my back, legs up on the beach, head down in the sea. Legs waving in the air, trying to find a way to stand up, trying unsuccessfully to reach my flip-flops while shooting water out of both nostrils.

Not going there again.

September

IN OUR GREEK VILLAGE

My birthday.
MY GREEKLISH FAMILY

What do you give the man who has everything for his birthday? How about a belly dancer?

We had to spend a few weeks at our home in England for a little business. We invited a few friends over for a birthday barbecue prior to flying back to Greece.

I wonder what possessed her to give me a gift-wrapped belly dancer as a present? I would have preferred a *bouzouki* player, or a bottle of my favourite *ouzo*.

No, she knew better. She decided it was appropriate to give me – an English man, married to a Greek wife – a Middle Eastern belly dancer, who had never been to Greece, dancing to Turkish music in an English country garden.

PETER BARBER

I think it was revenge for me giving her a cement mixer on her last birthday to lay the patio in our Greek village house.

I had better just buy her flowers next year.

Horses bite!

Alex, being a Greek city girl, is not used to life on the island. We were driving through Evia when Alex yelled.
"Stop the car!"

I was quite used to these demands. She is a keen Facebook user and loves to post photographs daily. I can never drive for more than a mile without a demand to stop because she has spotted a herd of goats, or a pleasant view. So, seeing some wild ponies in a meadow beside the road, she was keen to meet them.

Her previous experience with horses was limited to a quick pony ride up the hill in Santorini. But she had never met a wild horse. This was her chance.

As she opened the car door, I pulled her

back to explain how to approach them. As a country boy in the UK, I was used to horses and offered my advice.

I gave her a packet of mints from the glove compartment and held one in the flat of my hand.

"This is how you offer them the mint," I explained. "Hold it out in front of you and walk slowly towards them, but make no sudden moves. They will probably come towards you. When they take the mint, make sure it's in the flat of your hand, otherwise they may bite."

"Yeah, yeah, I know," she replied, and walked slowly towards them, holding the sweet. One lifted his head and its nostrils flared as it caught scent of the mint and walked towards her.

He put his velvet muzzle on Alex's hand and took the mint. Alex was delighted.

"Get the camera quickly," she demanded. "I need a photo."

I turned to retrieve the camera from the car and walk towards her and her new friend.

"Look," she said. "I don't need to hold the mint in my open palm. It enjoys being fed like this."

Before I could stop her, she held out a mint

in all five fingers and poked it into the pony's mouth. The pony bit down on the mint, and all of Alex's fingers, which were wrapped around the mint, and chewed.

The horse was spooked by Alex's screams and turned to run away, but her hand was still in its mouth. So there was Alex, running alongside the pony, trying to free her fingers while yelling for it to stop. After a few metres, it spat Alex out and ran towards the trees.

Her fingers were bruised and bleeding, so I drove her to the next village, where the pharmacist cleaned the wounds and bandaged her up.

"You shouldn't feed a horse that way," he explained and held out his hand flat to illustrate his point.

When we arrived in Pefki, our neighbour Maria arrived. Asked why her fingers were bandaged, Alex explained.

"You shouldn't feed a horse that way. It will bite you." She held out the flat of her hand. "This way is the right way."

I kept quiet. I hate to say I told you so.

Don't mess with the customs officer.

Alex, my dear Greek wife, is the reason for my writing career. An idea pops into her head, and she will do exactly what she wants, despite my words of caution. She is sparky and unpredictable, but has the kindest heart I have ever known.

Greeks are wonderful, open people. Formality is rare. We often fly to Athens airport from the UK. Usually, the customs hall does not include customs officers, but on this occasion, an official stopped me and asked me to open my bag. Alex stormed up behind me.

"Leave him alone, he's with me," she yelled in Greek.

The officer stood back and let us through with a smile and mumbled an apology.

Sometimes I watch as Alex speaks to tax inspectors, police officers or the local mayor in the same tone and Greek slang she uses to her friends while enjoying a coffee. This is one thing I love about Greece.

But, this lack of formality sometimes gets us into hot water in other countries. Istanbul was a challenge. We managed to get into the country after being interviewed vigorously, and having our luggage scanned twice. Alex was on her best behaviour that day, mostly because she had seen the tanks and soldiers on the runway, and a line of armed police directing us to the customs point.

But when we came to leave, it was a different matter. I stood at passport control and handed over my documents. The officer looked and shook his head.

"Big problem," he said. "Go to the police desk."

I had visions of the movie, Midnight Express. Being dragged off to a Turkish prison for some unknown offence. Perhaps they had found that bag of oregano that I got at the spice market the previous day. I did hope it really was oregano.

Alex could see me looking nervous, and her Greek protective instinct took over. She pushed past the barrier, and two armed police officers to confront the official holding my passport.

"He's done nothing wrong. Let him pass," she yelled as she thumped her fist on the desk.

The police officers stepped towards us and raised their guns. Luckily, the passport officer waved them away and explained the passport wouldn't scan, so the police had to just enter the numbers.

Recently we drove from Greece to the UK. At the UK passport control in Calais, Alex decided she would like a photograph of the nice lady sitting in the box.

"Put your camera away," I told Alex. "You're not allowed to take photos here."

"But I just want a photo of the flags," she replied.

As we stopped at the passport control, Alex leaned over me and called through my window to the officer.

"Can I take a photo please?"

"No photographs here," the officer replied and pointed to a large sign with a red line running through the image of a camera.

Alex started to protest, so I took her camera off her, flung it on the back seat and quickly drove away before we were both arrested.

MUSINGS FROM A GREEK VILLAGE

It's an exciting life, but I wouldn't have it any other way.

How to upset a Greek tortoise.

I love tortoises. In the summer, they wander freely around our garden chewing at the plants and shrubs. Most days I hand-feed them with a juicy slice of tomato.

It can be a risky existence for the tortoise. The cats just ignore them and pretend they don't exist. But one day, I saw one of our dogs sitting on the lawn. She was eating something, so I went to investigate. She was there with a small tortoise held in her paws, happily chewing around the edge of the shell, trying to get inside. Luckily, I got there before the main course.

At the veterinary clinic, there was a guy with a poorly looking dog curled up at his feet.

A pleasant lady with an unidentified creature wrapped in a blanket, a young boy with a goat on a piece of string, and me with a nibbled tortoise, all waiting for the vet.

The vet declared my patient fit and healthy with no lasting damage, so after a few days of convalescence in a box, I drove him to the mountains and left him with a packed lunch of sliced tomatoes and lettuce.

Often during our drives in the hills, I find one on the main road ambling across the tarmac. I always stop the car, pick it up and carefully place it in the nearby field.

The problem is that I don't know where they have been, or where they intend to go. I just don't want them to get run over, so I pick a side of the road and leave them there, but every time I get it wrong. As soon as I have placed him on the grass verge, he decides this is not the side of the road he wants to be on, and turns around and crosses the road again. I was sure they were just being difficult, or playing a game with me.

So, one day, I tested my theory.

I found a tortoise in the middle of the road. I picked him up and put him on one side. He crossed again. So I picked him up and put him on the other side. He didn't like that either and turned around and went towards the other side. This went on for a few more moments until I realised. He just wanted to be in the middle of the road.

I think that's why they are becoming rare.

Secrets revealed.

I am sitting at my desk writing my new book. My wife is in the next room quietly planning my day. I am busy writing a chapter about how we came to buy land on a Greek island. Suddenly, the world makes sense. My wife is a hypnotist.

Being married to a Greek, and writing about Greece, is a perfect combination. There is so much about living here that makes me smile every day. It's a journey of slow realisation of how things work. I am only just beginning to understand that I am married into a culture secretly controlled by wives who have, over countless generations, moulded the minds of men and created a better world despite our efforts to balls everything up.

Right from the start, mothers and wives programme us. We are assured that our word is law and we are the master of our home and family. Once we believe that, their job is done.

We men think we make all the decisions. They lead us to believe that we are in control. But it's their clever secret handed down from mother to daughter. They have developed an incredible and unfathomable way of planting the right idea into our heads and making us think we thought of it while praising us for being so clever. I used to watch my mother-in-law sweetly tie my father-in-law in knots with every important aspect of their lives while showering him with praise for his intelligence in making the right decisions.

I have only just realised my wife has the same genes.

"I know you have always wanted a house on an island," she sweetly whispered in my ear one day.

A few days later, she sowed the seed.

"Oh look, that piece of land is for sale and it's really cheap. What a coincidence. We were only talking about that a few days ago."

So, on my own and with no influence from anyone, I decided to buy some land and struggle with mind-bending bureaucracy for two years while almost putting myself into the poorhouse trying to build a house. I was determined to finish it, though. After all, it was my decision.

    I think I will stop writing now. I suddenly need to mow the lawn, dig over the garden and take my wife shopping for a new dress. I have no idea how I thought of that …

Greece is a lovely country, but why is everything uphill?

Alex knows I don't enjoy climbing. But it seems that every excursion around Greece includes climbing up mountains, rocky hills or thousands of steps. Perhaps it's my perception, but we always seem to go up, rarely down.

We have been to Nafplio. It was early in our relationship, and I was keen to impress my new wife. She decided it would be nice to visit the castle. I stood looking up at our destination and decided to talk her out of that idea.

"Look. It's a superb view of the castle from that *taverna* over there," I tried.

"It's a better view from up there looking

down," she replied. "And you will get a really good view of the sea from the castle," she assured me.

I tried again. I thought I would try chivalry this time.

"But it looks high. You may get afraid of the height," I suggested. She just looked at me and smiled ironically.

I thought about inventing a leg pain, or an old sporting injury received while playing rugby against the big boys. But I thought that may make me sound like a wimp, not the impression I wanted to give to my Greek goddess wife. I was trying to cultivate the image of an athletic, virile specimen of manhood. So, not being able to think of a good excuse which would also serve that purpose, I reluctantly agreed to climb the nine hundred and ninety-nine steps to the castle.

It was a hot day. After the first eighty-nine steps, I lost count. Sweat was pouring into my eyes, blurring my vision. Alex was ahead of me, bouncing up the steps two at a time, pointing at interesting flowers, and stopping occasionally to admire the view and let me catch up.

Halfway up I was suffering. The water bottle was empty, and I was finding it difficult to lift my feet for another step. Just before expiring from exhaustion, I sat on a step and pretended to gaze in wonder at the panorama below. Alex bounded back down and sat beside me.

"Are you OK?" she asked, "You look hot."

"I'm fine," I lied. "Just admiring the view."

I was fully dehydrated by the time we reached the castle. Alex was fine and looked fresh and cool. My hair was stuck to my forehead. The colour of my shirt had changed from white to a mucky sweat-stained brown. My face felt like I had stuck it in an oven.

But I had made it.

"The view?" asked Alex, raising her eyebrows.

Unfortunately, I was not focusing on the beauty and the grandeur of the historic castle.

I was focusing on the bloody car park next door.

Philosophy for all. Like it or not.

A lex is a true Greek philosopher. She is open and honest with everyone she meets. When we are in England, she often gets herself into trouble because some people mistakenly assume her to be rude. This is not the case. She has never learned the art of diplomacy. Most people find her openness attractive and refreshing, but others have no idea how to take her vibrant personality. Greeks express themselves in different ways.

"I'm not shouting, I'm Greek!"

In Athens, it is common for friends to disagree and fight with each other, then part as friends again. But in England, the system is more complicated. It's rare for a stranger to discuss anything deeper than the weather while keeping a respectable distance in case you invade their space. In Greece, no subject is taboo. So Alex brings Greece with her ...

When Alex asks you how you are, she really wants to know. She has a way of seeing a problem where there seems to be none. She will invade your space and slowly pick away at your shell until the truth is exposed.

Most of us try to show a calm surface to others. We are unwilling to open up and release our true feelings. But Alex can see below our calm village pond. She will see the old bicycle frames and discarded supermarket trolleys hidden below the surface. She will then help you drain your pond, and refill it with clear fresh water.

This is the Greek way. But it is something we are not used to.

I lost my old bike frames years ago, thanks to Alex. Still working on the discarded supermarket trollies though.

Boats hate me

Living in a Greek fishing village, it was only logical that I joined in the local pastime of fishing. So, I got myself a small boat with a trailer.

After a few months of splashing around in the sea, I had so far only caught one sardine and an anchor.

But if I was bad at fishing, my boating skills were much worse. The only place to launch it was the village slipway, which happened to be next to the *kafenio* where all the real fishermen sat together to drink coffee. After a few weeks of watching me getting tangled up trying to reverse my trailer down the slipway, and often finding myself hauling the waterlogged boat from the sea floor because I forgot to put the plugs in, I became rather well known as the worst sailor in the village and great entertainment.

So, I decided on another approach. I convinced myself that I wasn't a bad sailor. I just got nervous with all eyes on me and howls of laughter coming from the old men of the village. This was why I kept sinking my boat.

I decided to give my boat a rest and bought a small inflatable dinghy with a six-horsepower engine. My thinking was that I could launch from the nearby beach, so nowhere near the harbour. I would have no eyes on me. The villagers would be disappointed, but perhaps this way, my boating skills would improve.

Day one. I pumped it up, fixed the engine, pushed myself away from the beach and motored out to sea. I was about a mile offshore when the engine spluttered and cut out. Out of petrol. Luckily, I had a full can, so I topped up the tank and tried to restart the engine. After pulling at the starter cord for twenty minutes, it still refused to start. I rowed home.

Next day, same again. I got a mile out. Engine died, rowed home.

Day three. Got a mile out. Engine stopped, rowed home again.

So, I got a secondary petrol tank and linked

it to the engine so I wouldn't run out again. Got a mile out. The engine stopped, but this time, the wind had increased and was pushing me out to sea faster than I could row back.

There I was, furiously rowing against the wind, but the wind was winning as I watched the beach disappear. I began to panic. But I was saved. A passing fishing boat saw my struggles and came alongside, tossed me a rope and towed me to the harbour. News had already spread. The *kafenio* was packed with locals awaiting my arrival, with smiles on their faces.

One of the fishermen came over, lifted my engine cover, and secured the cooling pipe. Being a new engine, I should have connected this before I used it. Every time I took the boat out, the engine overheated and cut out.

My reputation as the worst sailor in the village was confirmed. Time for a new hobby.

October

IN OUR GREEK VILLAGE

Greek wine. It's an acquired taste.

Wine is such an interesting subject. We have often travelled through Europe and stayed at lovely hotels nestled amongst vineyards, all with their own special growing region and label. We have been tempted by vintage champagne in Reims. Red wines of Burgundy with their bottles emblazoned with beautifully printed labels sporting gold medals. Fruity chardonnay served in lime green bottles in silver antique ice buckets.

A *sommelier* is on hand to guide you through the flavour, and which one goes best with your chosen food. Most of the time, a bottle of wine will cost much more than your meal.

Then you arrive in Greece.

At the local *taverna* near our home, the wine list is different. The choice is a little simpler than a French *chateau* hotel and is confined to two. Red or white. We don't need a wine waiter to advise on which wine goes with which food. They both go with everything.

Here, everyone makes wine. Most *tavernas* make their own; even the local butcher sells his homemade brew. Glass bottles are rarely used. The wine is made and poured into 1.5-litre water bottles and sold for around one euro a litre.

I love Greek wine and drink nothing else while in Greece. Most of the time, this wine is excellent. But sometimes you need to work on developing a taste for a particularly challenging vintage.

George has a restaurant near our house and is proud of his wine. The only problem is it tastes like disinfectant. George likes to be traditional and makes wine the old Greek way, with pine resin, and a high alcohol content. We know this throughout the world as *retsina*. So, George makes his wine, and adds extra resin.

The only challenge is getting past the first glass. The first sip hits the back of your jaw like a hammer. You feel you have poured concentrated lemon juice into your mouth as it causes a shooting pain just below your earlobes.

Then the burn starts.

As you gather the confidence to swallow, your throat tries to close to protect itself. You must resist your body's gagging instinct to rid itself of this interesting flavour, but you must persist. As you swallow the first mouthful, a fire starts to run down your throat and settles on your chest.

First-time visitors to George's restaurant usually assume they are suffering a heart attack at this point, but it soon fades away, leaving you sweating and disoriented.

Once you have suffered the first glass, however, the next one tastes wonderful. It has stripped away your taste buds and even George's food tastes good. Perhaps that's his plan.

I always take visiting friends to George's restaurant. People need to feel the real Greece.

Peace and quiet in our village.

Our village is quiet. The silence is only broken by the rustle of leaves through the trees and the sweet summer sound of cicadas singing their daytime song, the crickets adding to the symphony once the sun goes down. Or perhaps the bleat of a goat on the nearby hillside and the odd passing fisherman calling out *"Psaria, psaria"* (fish, fish) as he walks through the village selling his catch. The restaurants and beaches are busy this time of year but out of earshot of our small hamlet in our medieval village.

That is because we are not there.

We travel a lot. So, when we leave to go on our travels, the village seems to breathe a collective sigh of relief. Peace at last. No more being woken by the buzz of chainsaws as Alex does a spot of pruning, or the regular revving as I test my dodgy boat engine. No more music turned up in the garden so I can hear it over the sound of Alex mowing the lawn with a bulldozer. Or loud Latino beats three times a day, accompanied by Alex's Zoom Zumba sessions.

But after we've been away for a week or two, the messages begin to arrive from our neighbours. They are getting bored. I had a message from Helen this morning, who lives opposite our home.

"When are you coming back? It's far too quiet here," she wrote.

Alex and I are like the hiccups of the village. They get on your nerves when you have them, but somehow miss them when they're gone.

Don't worry, Helen. We will be back soon.

How to become more Greek: Lesson 1.

Today's musing is to educate anyone who is thinking of visiting Greece. Greek food is the best in the world, so you must taste as much of it as possible. In tourist areas, restaurants catering for visitors have adopted the English way of serving food. This includes menus with pictures of food.

Menus are rare in real Greek *tavernas*. The waiter will either stand, or more likely, sit at your table to explain the best food today. Often he will invite you into the kitchen to choose for yourself.

A meal at our local *taverna* will start this way.

We find our table. George, the owner, will appear and put a jug of wine with three glasses on our table. He will pour himself one, take a sip, and briefly screw up his face before putting the glass down on the table.

"*Kalimera*, Petros and Alexandra. What are you eating today?" he asks.

"You told us yesterday you were going to make *kokoras krassatos*," (*coq au vin*) Alex said. "We will have that."

A sad look spreads over his face.

"Yes, that was the plan, but I couldn't catch him this morning. Maybe tomorrow."

"What about the *kouneli stifado?*" (rabbit stew) I asked.

"Sorry, he ran away. I have some nice fish though."

So, George went on to describe the fish and other specials of the day. We ordered a selection of dishes with our usual Greek salad.

In Greek restaurants, everybody shares. You must get out of the habit of ordering individual meals. After all, you would all share a bottle of wine. Why not share the food too?

We call this *meze*. They place food in the centre of the table, and they give each diner a small empty plate to fill as they wish.

Greek culture is built on food and hospitality. Eating is always a social event. A meal will last at least two to three hours, so as all dishes are shared, the lack of formality builds up a convivial feeling for all.

But, when Greeks eat together in a restaurant, the meal usually ends with an argument. Who is going to pay? If you are a visitor, it is unthinkable for a Greek to allow you to pay. It's a point of honour. So many times, I have felt embarrassed and sneaked off to pay before the meal ended, only to be told by the owner that he would not accept my money as he would be in trouble if he did. All Greeks want to be the host. By paying for everyone, that honour is achieved.

I have worked out the solution to this problem now. I just send Alex with the cash. It would be a brave *taverna* owner who would refuse her.

Next time you visit a Greek restaurant. Give the menu back and invite the waiter to share a glass of wine to chat about the food or ask to go into the kitchen to choose. Don't order individual portions. Just go Greek.

You won't regret it.

Alex shines in Chicago.

Yesterday was interesting. We joined a radio discussion on WCPT820 RADIO in Chicago to chat about our book. It was a one-hour slot hosted by Art Andros & Bobby Drell.

Bobby innocently asked the first question.

"Has Alexandra taught you any Greek?"

A trip to the local shops to buy bread would result in tears of laughter from the baker after asking for *psoli* (penis) instead of *psomi* (bread). I never returned to any Greek bakers after that experience. Asking the petrol pump attendant to fill me up, rather than the car. I soon realised that Alex probably wasn't the best teacher, and perhaps I needed to learn Greek elsewhere.

Many years ago, Alex's mother did warn me about her sparky daughter.

"She is a poet," she told me. "When she opens her mouth, diamonds and pearls are released."

I understood nothing of Greek language at that time, so I was blissfully unaware. But as I began to learn Greek, her fruity language became clear. Being proficient at English too, she also had mastered the art of English swearing, so when upset, I am subjected to a wonderful mix of Greek/English profanities, true Greeklish.

Art and Bobby must have been aware of Alex's reputation and pleaded with Alex to keep it clean, but just in case, they kept their fingers firmly on the bleep button.

It was an interesting show.

How to become more Greek: Lesson 2.
GREEK HIGHWAY CODE

Driving in Greece is a challenge. You need to remember that you may be the only person on the road who has actually passed a driving test.

Sharing the road with someone who has no idea of the rules makes driving an interesting experience. Motorbike riders don't even pretend to obey any rules. They only wear crash helmets in the winter to keep their heads warm. They are far too hot to wear in the summer.

In the interests of becoming more Greek, I have listed a few rules which will assist you while driving:

1. Hand signals in Greece are different. In England or the USA, if we want to say thank you, we hold our hand up. In Greece, it's an insult to show your palm. It doesn't mean thank you. Irate drivers will return the compliment with other, more graphic hand signals.
2. A Greek driver does not understand that there may be other people on the road and will never look behind them. They only use mirrors for makeup or hair combing.
3. Mountain roads are dangerous. Barriers intended to prevent you from plummeting to your doom are usually missing; in their place will be miniature churches on stilts, reminding you it would be a good idea to slow down. Greek drivers have a habit of parking halfway around a blind bend to admire the view, relieve themselves or take a selfie with the mountains as a backdrop.

4. Road signs are "advisory" for Greeks. Obeying a stop sign without checking your mirror will usually result in a motorbike inserting itself into your tailpipe.
5. Greeks dislike seatbelts. Most petrol stations will sell a clip that fits nicely into the belt mechanism to stop the annoying bleeping.
6. Speed limits in Greece are an infringement of civil rights and rarely taken seriously. The government did toy with speed cameras, but the blackened husks of these experimental devices, complete with oily rags around the pole, looked ugly, so they were discontinued in favour of planting some handsome new trees.
7. Be careful where you park. If you park illegally, the police will take your plates and it will cost one hundred and fifty euros to get them back. Paying the money is the simple part.
8. Zebra crossings are there for decoration only and not to be trusted. They serve no other

purpose. Greeks are fully aware of this, but tourists, assuming they have the right of way, take their lives in their hands. Cars seem to speed up as soon as you've placed one foot on the crossing.

9. In the UK, if a driver flashes his lights at you, it means he is giving way to you. In Greece, it means: "Get out of the way. I'm coming through."

10. Hazard lights do not mean that the vehicle is stopping or is in an emergency parking position. It means the driver is going to do something stupid. Maybe they're rolling a cigarette or just changing the radio channel.

How to become more Greek: Lesson 3.

DON'T COMMENT ON GREEK DRIVING.

I'm feeling a bit wounded today. My lovely Greek wife read my complaints about driving in Greece yesterday. Being a real Greek, with an even more Greek temperament, she took exception to my opinions about driving in Greece and assumed me to be seriously unpatriotic. Alex, like all Greeks, has the genes of Spartan warriors. But being female is much more dangerous. Luckily, I was not too badly hurt. The bandages should come off tomorrow, and the stitches are due to be removed next week. A narrow escape.

During my well-deserved assault, while pleading for mercy, I did, between blows from an expertly used *pantoúfle*, try in vain to point out that she was in the car with me and saw the driving.

This was not good enough.

Only Greeks who were born in Greece may make fun of Greek driving. Being married to a Greek, and living here for twenty-five years, doesn't count. As only an honorary Greek, I may watch, but must keep quiet.

I was thinking about writing a new piece about the mind-numbing bureaucracy next, but I am quite happy with my man bits and would really like to keep them.

I therefore end this musing by assuring everyone that Greek driving is the best in the world, (especially taxi drivers) and that nice lady that made my life hell for three days in the parking ticket department of Athens court, was only doing it in my best interest and is now my best friend. The flowers are on the way.

Is this OK, Alex? Please don't kill me.

Informality at the airport.

We recently arrived at Athens airport. As a Greek national, Alex skipped through the automatic passport control. I had to join the hour-long snake of foreigners queuing for the one open booth to receive my stamp before being let onto the hallowed turf of Europe. I too was now a foreigner. Brexit has a lot to answer for.

After the first thirty minutes, I had settled into dragging my feet, a brief step at a time, kicking my bag along the floor and breathing down the neck of the guy in front in case anyone might sneak ahead of me. It was almost silent in the hall. The only sound was from shuffling as the queue moved unbearably slowly, and the occasional click of stamps on passports.

Suddenly, there was an unfamiliar noise. Tap, tap, tap. It was Alex knocking on the passport booth window. The official was so shocked, he missed the passport he was currently stamping and tattooed the desk instead. He left his booth, and a whispered conversation ensued. Alex was talking quietly and pointing in my direction.

I was saved. Alex had felt sorry for me. My wait was over. I was going to receive VIP treatment. Soon I would be free. I was getting hot and bothered, and my legs were aching after a long flight. I dreamed of my first Greek coffee, which, thanks to my caring wife, would be at any moment. I stepped forward, waving my passport as they both approached me.

"Have you got one euro for the baggage trolley?" Alex asked.

I felt deflated as I reached into my pocket for a coin. Alex disappeared towards the baggage carousel. The official went back into his booth to continue his work, leaving me in the line. "Thanks, Alex," I muttered under my breath.

But, to Alex's surprise, she found it a little different at Heathrow. We approached passport control. Alex looked up and saw a Union Jack flag sticker pasted on a sign which read "Welcome to Border Control". Under this friendly sign was a sour-looking uniformed Home Office official ready to check our passports. Alex pulled her phone out of her bag to take a photograph.

"Stop!" the official yelled, and pointed to a "No Photograph" sign.

Alex was undeterred. She continued to fiddle with her phone.

"Madam. It is against the law to take photographs here. This is border control. You will be arrested."

In Greece, the immigration officer would probably join you in a nice selfie and likely ask you to WhatsApp a copy to him. Here, you are likely to be handcuffed and dragged away for interrogation, including an intimate body search and large quantities of Vaseline.

This was Alex's introduction to British culture, and so far, she was not impressed. I could feel the vibes of anger rising. She was getting ready for a fight she could not possibly win. I gripped her arm tightly.

Alex will follow rules, but only if they make sense. Not being allowed to drive though a red light makes sense. It could cause a tangled heap of wreckage, with you as part of it. Not being allowed to stuff fifty kilos of olive oil into your aircraft baggage makes sense. It's never a good idea to take highly flammable liquid and add that to the other fifty thousand kilos of jet fuel already on board. But not being able to take a photo of a flag made no sense at all.

"Please don't make a fuss," I pleaded. "Things are different here. You may get away with this in Greece, but here you must follow the rules. No photographs."

Alex nodded and put her phone away, but was still sulking as we went to collect our bags.

Happy memories of summer.

ALEX CHARMS VENICE.

Often, Alex and I travel to other countries and experience different cultures. This summer, we drove home to Greece through Europe. Alex took her Greek flag to wave proudly in every city visited, and it was a great success, but in Venice, we had a wild time.

We had a two-day stopover, so took the opportunity to walk around the beautiful narrow streets along countless canals opening into delightful squares. We attended a Vivaldi concert where Alex waved her flag enthusiastically in time with the music, drawing smiles and waves from the orchestra.

The last evening, we went for a walk around the world-famous St Mark's Square in the centre of Venice. There was a selection of pavement cafes spread around the perimeter, some with a piano player reciting classical music, others with a full orchestra. We had heard that this was the world's most expensive venue for coffee. But we were only in Venice for a short while, so decided to suffer the cost and sat down at a table.

The band was playing softly as we ordered our drinks and sat to enjoy the experience. Alex planted her Greek flag in a flower vase in the centre of the table.

The leader of the orchestra looked over at Alex and called:

"Are you from Greece?" he asked.

Alex nodded. Then the chap whispered to the band, and they began to play "Zorba the Greek".

Alex was delighted. She stood up, grabbed her flag and began to dance. Soon, a few others stood up from their tables and joined her. By the time the music ended, everyone who was in St Mark's Square had come over to our cafe and were clapping and cheering in time with the music.

MUSINGS FROM A GREEK VILLAGE

I'm not sure any other piece of music would have received the same response. People just love Greece.

Misunderstanding in Greece.

T he Greek language can be confusing. Especially, if like my younger brother, you only know the words taught to you by Alex. My brother had just returned from his Greek holiday with an angry look.

"Did you have a delightful time?" I asked.

"No, I bloody well did not," he replied. "I don't want to talk about it."

This was surprising. I would have thought he would have had a lovely time in this beautiful, warm and welcoming country. After a little probing, all became clear. My dear brother, along with thousands of other tourists, had learned his first Greek word.

Malaka is the most common word in the Greek language. Tourists learn it before they learn to say good morning. It's used with a variety of different meanings by men and women, but it literally translates as "man who masturbates".

While people typically use it as an insult, with its equivalent in English being "wanker", the meaning alters depending on the context. It can be an exclamation of pleasure, an expression of horror, a cry of anger, a declaration of affection, or something else entirely.

Finally, I got the story.

"On the last day of my holiday, I went to the *kiosk* to buy a packet of cigarettes and he called me a *malaka*," he explained. "I am never going to Greece again because they are rude."

Jon had fallen into the trap of the Greek tone. The chap in the *kiosk* had only asked him if he preferred a hard packet of cigarettes or soft (*mal-a-ka vs. malakó*).

The word is the same, but the pronunciation changes the meaning completely.

November

IN OUR GREEK VILLAGE

Irish coffee made difficult.

As winter approaches, we are now looking forward to the cold weather in Greece. This time of the year we usually think about driving to Arachova, then up the mountain to the Parnassos ski resort. Like most Greeks, we don't ski.

Our one and only attempt at skiing didn't end well. Alex and I decided to have a go, but soon found out that these long bits of wood on our feet had no brakes, and we ended up in a tangled heap of arms, legs and broken skis under the terrace of the cafe with bobble-hatted heads staring down at us with large grins on their faces. So, long ago, we decided to do the same as most people and laugh at someone else.

But we enjoy the cable car trip up the mountain, and the cafe at the top makes a good hot chocolate. So, we sit on the terrace, breathe in the clean, crisp air, and admire the view of the snowy mountain. We sip our hot drinks and watch the few skiers who manage to stay upright long enough slide down the mountain, but more often backwards or head first.

We had finished our first hot chocolate and went off to the bar for a refill. I looked above the counter and saw on the menu board: "Special Offer: Irish Coffee 2 euros." I love Irish coffee, so I ordered one.

The girl behind the counter looked at me with a blank expression. She obviously had no idea what Irish coffee was.

"Sorry, we're out of that," she informed me.

"OK, do you have whiskey?"

"Yes," she replied.

"You have coffee?"

"Of course, this is a coffee bar," she said, looking at me as if I were simple.

"Any cream?" I asked.

"Yes, lots."

"Okay. I will have a cup of coffee, a shot of whiskey, and cream on top."

"No problem," she replied.

She made the Irish coffee, set it on the counter, and started her calculations.

"That will be five euros for the whiskey, four euros for the coffee, and one and a half euros for the cream. That comes to ten euros and fifty cents."

I couldn't be bothered to argue. I had my Irish coffee.

Autumn in our village.

Our Greek island village is quiet. Tourists have left, there are no more crickets in the trees. Mosquitos have gone into hiding to wait for the long days of next summer when the feeding frenzy can begin again. Sunbeds have been cleared away from beaches and piled under tarpaulins to wait for next summer. Most of the *tavernas* have closed for the season. The ones still open service the locals and are warm and welcoming. The atmosphere is strangely calm after the record-breaking tourist season.

The grapes have been harvested, and the juice is quietly bubbling in thousands of home-made fermenting jars, ready to provide an interesting assault of the taste buds for next year's crop of tourists. My local *taverna* owner George is busy adding extra pine resin to his brew to make it extra special.

There is a heady aroma of home stills with steam puffing out of windows as the slow drip of the spirit *tsipouro*, is collected into vats ready to bottle as internal central heating for the old men of the village during the colder months.

Recently we went to buy some trees for the garden from the old man who grew them.

Suddenly Alex stopped, put her face near the man's and sniffed.

"Have you been drinking?" she asked accusingly. "You realise it's only nine a.m.?"

"Of course I've been drinking," he replied. "I make about a hundred litres of *tsipouro* every year. I can't sell it all, so I have to drink the rest, don't I?"

Sounds logical, I thought.

The old man is not alone. Any cafe or *taverna* in the village will have tables outside filled with local men chatting and drinking this dangerous spirit.

The bar owner will bring tiny bottles about the size of miniatures served during flights. It's common to see hundreds of the little empty bottles pushed to the centre of the table until the bar owner sweeps them into a wire shopping basket, takes them away and brings them back, filled.

One day, I visited a friend in the village. He asked if I would like to try his home-made booze.

"Okay, just a small one," I agreed.

He led me into the garden. There was a fifty-gallon green plastic drum covered with a black lid. He removed the cover and reached in, took a ladle, and poured a huge portion into a glass. It tasted like aniseed-flavoured fire.

A word of warning. Don't. Drink. *Tsipouro*. This strange Greek spirit is the big brother of *ouzo* and gets your feet drunk first. You could be enjoying a meal and a glass or two. Feeling relaxed and clear-headed until you try to stand up. The *tsipouro* has attacked your legs and given them a mind of their own. You try to walk one way, but your legs have decided to go somewhere else.

They make so much of this booze in the autumn, that it is common to see sober men staggering around the village, arguing with their own drunken legs.

I love living here.

A simple life in my Greek village.

When was the last time you met your neighbour? In The UK we lived in a small cul-de-sac and as far as we were aware, no one else lived nearby. There must have been people living in these houses because bins were emptied, and milk deliveries taken in and replaced with clean empty bottles. But we never met or heard any of these reclusive hermits.

People hide behind locked doors, shutting away the outside world. Sometimes you are lucky enough to receive a quick nod if you meet a neighbour rushing past. The art of communication is fast disappearing.

But not in my Greek village. Privacy is unknown. Here, everyone knows everyone.

We often arrive home to find our neighbour Maria sitting on our patio with another neighbour. Maria had been into the house and made coffee. At the same time she had given the floor a quick mop.

I love cooking and one day made the mistake of asking Maria how to cook *kokoretsi*, a traditional Greek dish. Most people would explain a recipe or scribble it on a piece of paper. Not Maria. She disappeared into the kitchen, rummaged around the fridge and cupboards, found the ingredients which I had purchased that morning and emerged onto the patio to prepare and cook it for us.

As the *kokoretsi* turned on the barbecue, the cooking smells attracted neighbours who had been walking past and came in to investigate. By the time it was ready, some of the neighbours had gone off and returned with salads, bread, wine and large bottles of *tsipouro* to add to the meal, then sat to join us. We ended up with fifteen people around the table chatting, drinking and enjoying lunch. All because I asked for a recipe.

It seems that the village knows more about me than I do. Alex's brother came to stay with us recently. As a Greek, he enjoyed his morning coffee with the old men in the local *kafenio*. He returned and told me that today I was the subject of the village gossip.

Apparently, I'm married to a nice foreigner (Athenian). Although Greek, anyone not born in the village is an outsider.

I'm a rich English lord with a castle in England who never rents his house to tourists because I don't need the money.

I am the worst fisherman they have ever seen and grow strange things in my garden that you can't eat and have terrible taste in hats. But although I do seem rather dim, I'm a nice guy.

I felt so complimented.

As it's Sunday, I thought I would change the tone a little.

Alex and I have just watched the film about the life of Saint Nectarios of Aegina. It was a great and powerful movie about a beautiful and peaceful man.

We have often visited his tomb on the island, the church of Agios Nektarios. It's a beautiful place which everyone should visit at least once.

Alex, my Greek wife, has a personal relationship with this holy man. When she was a small girl, she lived with her family in Glyfada, a short ferry ride from Aegina. Alex was always a sparky girl in the village and was responsible for a lot of the mischief in her street.

If a cat ran past with a tin tied to its tail, it was her. If a neighbour's fence had mysteriously disappeared, she had moved it to make a ramp for her bike so she could jump over things – usually, her brother, who she forced to lie on the road at the end of the ramp.

Whenever the parents of the local bully came to the house to complain about his injuries, Alex would hide her bruised knuckles behind her back and wear her cutest expression; they invariably left convinced of her innocence and cursed their own child for telling lies.

Her mother grew so worried about Alex's naughtiness that she took her to the local doctor, who declared that there was nothing physically wrong with her and suggested a priest.

The priest recommended a visit to the tomb of St Nectarios of Aegina. Alex's mother was a devoted Christian and took the priest's advice and booked ferry tickets for the next day.

Alex, more than happy to take time off school to visit the island, spent the day picking flowers from the grounds and being fussed over by the monastery's nuns.

She was taken into the chapel for an exorcism. She was quite content as she had armfuls of flowers from the gardens by now and needed to sit down for a while to arrange them in her hair and make flowery designs on her clothes. She just concentrated on the flowers while a priest read from a book and sprinkled her with holy water and oil.

But when they brought out the smoking incense burners, these made her cough. This was taken as a sign that the exorcism had succeeded and the demon expelled.

I have a feeling we need to return soon.

Greece is not perfect.

I had best keep writing in case Alex sees this headline.

Alex's brother lived in Holland. He arrived to stay with us for a holiday. For the first few days, he wandered around Glyfada, tutting with disapproval.

"In Holland, the trains and buses run on time, and they are spotlessly clean," he told Alex.

"The drivers here are terrible, the road signs make little sense, and where are the cycle lanes?"

He went on to criticise everything about Greece, from lack of organisation, stray cats and dogs, graffiti, and anything else that wasn't like Holland.

Alex sat and listened patiently without a flicker of her usual anger when her country is criticised.

I would never have got away with this. If I ever show the slightest disapproval of her beloved country, I am in real danger of physical harm, usually with her weapon of choice, a slipper or a mop, or even more scary, the laser-beam stare.

As a writer about Greece, I walk the tightrope daily, my written words carefully vetted to ensure I don't slip into the abyss. I recently wrote an article about Greek drivers. Although based on authentic life experience, my life was in danger until I wrote an apology, confirming I didn't really mean it.

So how come he could get away with it? He had not been hit, not once. She hadn't screamed at him or threatened his life. This was not her usual restraint. The only reason I could think of was she had made allowances for him living abroad and becoming institutionalised. After all, he was still Greek, and still her brother.

So, an uneasy peace fell upon the house. I could see Alex was upset and something needed to be done to lift the spirits in the house. So, on the third day of his visit, we helped him become Greek again, and took him to our home in northern Evia.

On the first day, he walked down to the harbour and joined the old men for coffee. When he returned, his expression had changed. He looked calm and peaceful. His eyes had opened to the beauty and the kindest people in the world around him. It was as if he had woken from a dream where everything in his life was organised and robotic.

Now, he was free. Now, he was Greek again.

Here, life is simpler. If you miss a bus, there's probably another tomorrow. Things run in a different time zone. People are more relaxed, there's no pressure to rush and keep appointments and everyone is happier for it.

Some European countries have become clinical and over-formal. The population will follow the rules. Don't cross the road if there is a red light. Take your place in the queue. Don't stand out from the masses; become part of the machine.

I lived and ran a business in England. Life was stressful and difficult. I lived in a rat race among other rats chasing an unknown dream.

Until I arrived in Greece, I had no idea what life could be like. But Greece and the wonderful Greek people showed me what life was really about.

Greece is an organised chaos which works. So, Greece is not perfect.

But for me, it is.

"Every heart sings a song, incomplete, until another heart whispers back." – Plato

I write every day. The beauty of Greece captivates my soul. But without someone to share it with, would I feel the same?

Alex and I share an appreciation of everything around us. I write a story; I cannot wait to share it with Alex.

She goes for a walk along the beach; when she arrives home, she can't wait to show me the photographs of something interesting she has found.

Two people with similar interests and love for each other complete the cycle of life, which makes us love everything around us. In this state of mind, we can look away from the minor irritations in life and fill our world with love and laughter.

But what about the people who have nobody to share with? Would I feel the beauty of my life if I were alone?

There are many people in this world who have no one to share with, through choice or otherwise. But we find true happiness in sharing. In the words of Plato: "Every heart sings a song, incomplete, until another heart whispers back."

Greek fishing adventures.
THAT ONE CAN KILL YOU!

Being a keen angler as a child, I passed many happy days pulling fish out of my local canal. Sometimes, if I was lucky, I would visit the seaside and even fish from a boat. I got to know all the fish species and caught many.

When I moved to Greece, being near the sea, I had the perfect opportunity to practise my angling skills in a new place without the British weather. I got a small boat and went a few hundred metres from the beach. I let out the line and waited. After a few moments, the line went taut, and I pulled up a small red fish. In an hour, I had a bucket full of small various coloured fish, none of which I recognised.

Some looked like the ones I had seen at the local market, so I assumed they were edible and took them home. Over the kitchen sink, I cleaned and descaled them, dipped them in flour and fried them in oil. They were delicious.

The next day, Demetris invited me to join him on his boat for a spot of fishing. He is a proper fisherman and knows his stuff. He would not give away his favourite fishing spot, so we just rowed out for a few moments to an area he knew where there were a few small fish which could be easily caught.

We sat bobbing around on the blue Aegean in the bright sunshine when I had the first bite. I pulled the fish over the side of the boat, and Demetris saw the fish and almost jumped into the sea with fright.

"Don't touch it," he screamed "it's dangerous."

The fish was about thirty centimetres long, with bright blue stripes along its flanks and a row of sharp-looking spikes along its back. I gently lifted it over the side and cut the line, letting it drop back into the sea.

Demetris sat back and visibly relaxed.

"That was a deadly poisonous fish. If it had stung, you could have died," he assured me.

MUSINGS FROM A GREEK VILLAGE

 I didn't like to admit that I had caught one yesterday. I took it home, cleaned it, and fried it with a few chips.
 It was delicious.

Living on a Greek island.

Sitting in my garden on summer evenings, the sound is beautiful. *Tzatzikis* and the cicada serenade us from the trees as we relax over an *ouzo*.

The local crickets add to the cacophony by rubbing their back legs together to make their music.

That is all except Eric. Eric is a cricket that moved in with us recently. He doesn't sing much as he only has one leg. Sometimes I watch as he waves his real leg around trying to rub it against his phantom limb, but without a sound. Eric is dumb. Shunned by other crickets, an outcast who had nowhere to go so he came to live with us.

Since living on the island I have never

looked for a pet. They just turn up and stay. We now have several cats prowling the garden, a stray dog that arrives for food most days, a mole living under my lawn, and a lizard without a tail who lives in the kitchen. Not to mention the herd of goats that wander through my garden every day.

    I love living here.

December

ON OUR GREEK ISLAND

The gang's all here.

We arrived in Pefki yesterday afternoon. As we took our bags from the car, the first cat arrived and wrapped his body around my legs as I tried to pull the suitcase through the door. I lifted my foot, trying to avoid standing on it, tripped, and a loud squeal announced the arrival of the second cat as I trod on its tail. By the time the car was unloaded, four cats were sitting on the porch waiting for lunch.

I was expecting this. Cats in our village have an elaborate messaging system. They all seem to know when the soppy Englishman is arriving, and the word spreads through the feline community. I think they have Wi-Fi.

I took the bag of Friskies from my suitcase

and went out to feed the four cats that had suddenly become six cats. By the time lunch was finished, the pack had grown to nine.

Apart from a few chewed ears, all of my friends seem to be in good condition and healthy. I think most of them must be owned, but the word has spread that we are the best restaurant in town, so scraps left out by our kind neighbours are ignored in favour of the exotic food source here.

At the moment, the count is twelve full-size moggies, and two kittens.

I think I need more cat food.

The little house on the hill.

Close to our home in northern Evia is a small village set on top of a hill with an incredible view of the Straits of Artemision, and the nearby island of Skiathos. We found it by accident while looking for a local *taverna* and took a wrong turn. The village comprises a small square with a few houses on each side. Dominating the square is the old *kafenio* which had been left to decay for many years.

It was love at first sight. It was a typical Greek house. Stone-built with blue/green shutters and flaking paint. It was perfect. There was a small garden to the side with orange trees heavy with fruit. The building was intact, but clearly in need of loving care. I pushed at the door and stepped inside. The old timber floor had rotted, and weeds grew around the perimeter. There was no staircase, so the upper floor needed to be entered from the rear. But the gate was firmly locked, so we couldn't see that.

I suggested to Alex that I could buy it. It could be a hobby project. I could do the work myself and make it into a nice little house for visiting friends.

Alex, being used to my crazy ideas, saw an opportunity to get me away from the house and keep me occupied so readily agreed. She was sure that this idea would pass as soon as my building skills caused the house to fall down during my attempted renovations. We could always use the stones and build a rockery in our garden.

We asked around the village and tracked down the owner. He was willing to sell, and the price asked was unbelievably low, a little more than the cost of a second-hand car, so I held out my hand to shake on the agreement.

Before taking my hand to seal the deal, he mentioned a minor problem.

"I hope you will allow Ivan the Bulgarian to stay. He's lived upstairs for years."

"Does he pay rent?" I asked.

"No," he replied. "He just helps around the

village, picks grapes and olives in the autumn, takes on odd jobs here and there."

This revealed why the house was so cheap. If I was to buy it, then Ivan came with the deal. I still pass the house sometimes, but I've never met the mysterious tenant. We decided it was unkind to subject Ivan to my building skills while he was living upstairs. It would probably be dangerous. So, I abandoned the whole idea and went home to think about a different project that wouldn't upset my wife too much.

For me, this typified the kindness of Greeks. The owner of this old house was more interested in the welfare of the chap who made it his home, than turning a profit. Some things are more important than money.

I love living here.

My Greek wife is trying to kill me.

Those of you who have read my first book will be aware how Alex tried to tip us off a mountain ravine as a joke. We narrowly survived that adventure.

But Alex hadn't finished yet and had decided to electrocute me.

The jasmine at the front of the house was getting overgrown and looking a little untidy, so Alex set about cutting it. She was snipping away happily with the shears, when there was a spark, and all the power in the house went out. She had severed the cable to the outside lights.

"No problem," I told her, "it's an easy repair."

I found scissors and electrical tape and went outside to assess the damage. It was a clean cut, so would be easy to join. I found the switch on the wall amongst the various light switches and turned off the light circuit. The power in the house came back on, leaving the garden lights without electricity.

I looked at the cable. I'm OK with wiring a plug, but I was used to dealing with wires of a different colour. In the UK, brown means live. Blue means neutral. Here they were multi-coloured stripy wires and most confusing. I had a little screwdriver with a light in the handle to tell me which wire was live, but needed to turn it on.

"Alex, switch the power on," I called.

Alex flicked the switch. I tested each wire and found the live one.

"Okay, switch it off," I shouted.

Alex switched it off.

I didn't have a wire stripper, so decided to use my teeth. I put the cable in my open mouth, ready to bite. Then had second thoughts. I called to Alex.

"Are you sure the power is off?" I asked.

"Yes, of course," Alex assured me.

I put the cable back in my open mouth, but before biting down, I thought I should check for myself. I went into the house and looked at the switches. Alex had turned off the wrong one. The wire I was just about to bite was still live.

A few days later, Alex wanted a chandelier put up. Because I had successfully repaired the outside wire without blowing my head off, she was sure I could do it.

Two problems presented themselves.

First, it was a really high ceiling. Second, I didn't fancy experimenting with electrics again.

But Alex insisted she had faith, so I reluctantly agreed.

This time I turned the power off at the mains and climbed the ladder with my electric drill, which didn't work because the power was off. I came down, switched the power on and climbed the ladder. I drilled a hole, came down and turned the power off.

Back up the ladder, the hole wasn't deep enough. Came down, switched on the power, back up the ladder, drilled the hole deeper, came down, switched off the power, back up the ladder, I forgot my screwdriver.

Back down the ladder, power back on, got the screwdriver, went up the ladder, touched the wire, I went bang and lit up like a Christmas tree.

I'm not doing that again.

Our little village, Glyfada.

It's good to be home. We arrived in Glyfada on Wednesday, a little tired after our trip. We delayed going to our island home while we caught up with a few friends.

Glyfada has changed a little more. A few extra shops have opened, others have closed. The malls are strangely quiet this year; Christmas shopping seems on hold.

Our first visit was opposite our home, to see Stella. Alex remembers her from her childhood when the street was populated by small ramshackle houses and a packed earth road. Now it's a wealthy street full of apartment blocks and upmarket restaurants.

Stella lives on the top floor of her apartment block, which is built on the land her old house used to stand on. She used to be the street's chicken and egg supplier. Now she just lives with her cats well above the street.

No one sees Stella any more. Gone is her loud foghorn voice yelling greetings up and down the street. Gone are the chickens that used to populate her front garden.

Alex pressed her bell. An incoherent crackle came from the intercom before the door buzzed and opened. We stepped into the small elevator and pressed the button for the top floor.

Stella opened her door and a waft of cat smell assaulted us as she stood at her door wearing an old nightgown reaching to just above her knobbly knees, with bare feet and a mop of unruly grey hair. But her smile was beautiful and her eyes were full of tears. I looked at Alex, who also had tears running down her cheeks. Stella was a remnant of her happy childhood, bringing more happy memories flooding back ...

We gave her some gifts we had brought from England; some chocolate and tea bags.

"Did you bring any slippers?" she asked. "I need slippers."

"Yes," Alex lied, feeling sorry for her barefooted friend. "But I left them at home. I will go and get them."

Back in the lift, Alex and I were now on a mission. We needed to find some slippers. We stepped onto the street for the short walk to the mall. Suddenly, there was a voice behind us.

"*Yiasou*, Peter and Alexandra!"

We turned to see another of our old neighbours hurrying to catch up with us. We stood and chatted for a few moments before bidding her goodbye. A few seconds later, we passed the local travel agency. Danos came running out of his shop, flung his arms around us both, and hugged us in welcome. More tears flowed as we exchanged memories before we continued our walk.

What would normally be a five-minute walk from our home to the shoe shop took over an hour. We met friends, wishes were given and memories were exchanged. We chose three pairs of slippers. Another hour later, we arrived back at Stella's house after meeting more old friends, drinking coffee and feeling like we had never left.

To the outsider, Glyfada looks like a gentrified city. People no longer live in small houses with fruit trees in their gardens and chickens running freely around the street.

But the true heart of the city still beats below the surface.

To us, it's still our village and these are our people.

Good afternoon Greece.

Recently, I was having a chat over the fence with a similar-aged Greek neighbour (keeping two metres apart) comparing our early lives. I found myself talking about the young people of today, and how they don't know how good they have it. Starting sentences with: "In my day," and "When I was young."

Bugger. I must be getting old.

My wife Alex grew up in this wonderful place when there were still houses and earth roads. She watched the town spread sideways and upwards until it became a city filled with multi-story apartment blocks and designer shops.

I was born and raised in England in the

1960s and didn't discover the wonders of Greece until later when I met my beautiful wife.

So, for you younger people out there, I will give you a little British history lesson.

When I Was Young:

• The only takeaway food was fish and chips. Pizza hadn't been invented yet, even Colonel Sanders hadn't heard of Kentucky Fried Chicken. McDonald's didn't exist, and Wimpy was a character from Popeye the Sailor Man. Olive oil was only available from chemists to remove earwax, and also was Popeye's girlfriend.

• Garlic was disgusting and made you smell, pasta came in tins, and the only herbs that we knew about were parsley and mint. Only rich people had chicken, steak was only used to cover your black eye, beer was served warm and the only flavour of crisps available was plain or cheese and onion.

• Pornography was only found in smutty magazines but always out of reach in the newsagent. If you found a second-hand one, the pages were always stuck together. The world wide web was something to do with exotic spiders, and Facebook was a black-and-white photo album.

• Smoking was encouraged. We had to learn to roll a cigarette before we could walk. Central heating was a two-bar electric fire. Frost would only appear on the inside of windows, and you would only get one bath a week.

• Entertainment on TV consisted of two channels. It started at 6.00 p.m. with the news, then *The Black and White Minstrel Show* (in black and white). Alf Garnett, and *Muffin the Mule*, which was banned (ask your grandad). We looked forward to documentaries showing women in other parts of the world with no clothes on. This was always shown late (about 9.00 p.m.) as it was a little rude. TV shows ended with the national anthem at 10.00 p.m. when we all had to stand up and salute the Queen. We used to wait for the little white dot to fade on the screen before we went to bed.

• Homosexuality was illegal. Gay meant happy. Sexual predators were accepted, as every village had its dirty old man that your mother told you to keep away from. You just learned to not kick your football into his garden as getting it back was a challenge. Jimmy Savile was still a DJ. If we had known that he had other hob-

bies, we would never have kicked our ball into his garden.
- Sex education had something to do with beekeeping, which I never fully understood.
- Vegetarians were usually rabbits, never humans. We just ate what we were given and thought it was our birthday if we found some meat in our gruel.

In My Day:

- Schools still had inkwells. These were pots of dark liquid used to dip sharp sticks into, allowing you to scratch paper and leave interesting ink blot patterns later utilised by psychiatrists to judge your level of insanity.
- The only qualification needed to get a teaching degree was to become proficient at sadism. They all carried a cane and used it to beat you half to death when caught being naughty. Naughty things included: talking in class, running in the corridor, dogs eating homework, and looking at teachers the wrong way, not looking at teachers while being brutalised, and having an opinion or, in my case, dyslexia. This was designed to enforce discipline and mould your brain to accept without question any crap spoon-fed to you.

- The national curriculum focused on core subjects such as maths, English, and the history of the British Empire. Mostly trying to brainwash us into believing in our dominance over any race in the world that was not us. We were shown maps of the empire showing countries we had invaded, and kept. We were told that Johnny Foreigner could not be trusted, as he wasn't one of us.

Fast Forward to 23 June 2016.

It is well known that the older population of the United Kingdom overwhelmingly voted for Brexit. Now you know why. As kids, we were taught racism, sexism and nationalism since we could walk. Some of us rebelled against our formal education and grew an additional brain cell. Some didn't, and just passed the prejudices onto their kids.

Slowly, though, the world is changing. I spend most of my time in Greece with these lovely people and love every moment. But it's nice to remember, as it makes me appreciate what I have now even more.

Thank you, Greece.

Life in a Greek island village.

I woke up to the sound of scraping on my bedroom window and tinkling bells. I pulled on my dressing gown and sleepily looked out of the window. A large goat looked back at me. He was standing upright with his front hoofs tapping on the glass. I opened the door to the garden, and he watched me suspiciously as I stepped onto the patio. Rubbing the sleep from my eyes, I patted him on the head and wished him good morning. A voice came from further away.

"*Kalimara.*"

There was a shepherd waving. He was holding a long staff with a small white dog sitting by his side with its tongue lolling out of the corner of its mouth. Scattered around my garden, there was an entire flock of goats happily munching on my land.

"*Kalimera?*" I replied. (Coffee?)

"Yes. five sugars, no milk," he replied. "And some cheese with a little bread."

So, I went back into the house to make his coffee and cheese sandwich while wondering why he had brought his flock of goats to visit. Perhaps he was trying to sell me some?

Soon I was back in the garden with his breakfast. I didn't ask why he had decided to visit. I was just happy to see them. So I complimented him on his goats and discussed the weather while he sipped his coffee, finished his sandwich and wandered away with his flock close behind. What a lovely way to start the day.

If I had known they were coming, I wouldn't have cut the lawn yesterday.

The Greek monkey who changed history.

L et's go to the zoo, Alex suggested.
I had no idea there was a zoo in the centre of Athens – this was certainly news to me.

Alex led me across the busy road into the National Gardens, next to the parliament building. The contrast to the city was incredible. Traffic noise had disappeared, to be replaced by birdsong. We walked through the trees, past a pond, and arrived at a section of animal cages.

We walked hand in hand past the first few, peeking inside to see the animals. But there weren't any. Every cage was empty, until we came across one at the very end, containing a bored-looking goat accompanied by two fluffy rabbits hopping around the enclosure.

"So, this is Athens zoo?" I asked Alex. "There are not many animals."

"Yes. We did have a bear, but it died," she told me. "But we have some ducks."

She waved her hand towards the pond where two brown ducks were paddling around on the surface. "We used to have more, but I think they got eaten."

Another zoo near Athens was the summer palace of King Alexander. The area is a densely wooded, south-east-facing slope of Mount Parnitha.

On 30 September 1920, King Alexander was walking with his dog through the park and was bitten by a monkey. He succumbed to sepsis three weeks later. His death was followed by the restoration of his deposed father, King Constantine I, the ousting of prime minister Venizelos, and the reshuffling of the country's military leadership: events that ultimately led to the Asia-Minor Catastrophe of 1922. Commenting on this sequence of events, Winston Churchill wrote:

"It is perhaps no exaggeration to remark that a quarter of a million persons died of this monkey's bite."

Everywhere in the incredible city of Athens has a story. You just need to look below the surface.

These zoos are now closed, but a brand-new one has been built near the airport. I think the goat and two bunny rabbits live there now.

I don't want a swimming pool.

I have actually spoken to people who visited Greece and have asked them if they enjoyed it. I am always keen to hear stories of their impression of my beautiful adopted country. But I am often disappointed.

"Yes, the pool was wonderful, the weather was glorious," is the usual reply.

They had spent two weeks wandering between the hotel bar, restaurant and pool. They didn't set foot outside their hotel, but had a wonderful time. Greece, Spain, Turkey or any other sunny European resort could have been their location. Would they have known the difference?

Asked when asked why they chose Greece

for this adventure; the reply is usually, "Because I love Greece."

But the only part of Greece they had seen was the route from the airport to the hotel, and back again two weeks later.

Many hotels have realised this and anticipated the needs of these travellers. Fully self-inclusive hotels are arriving. These fully insulate travellers from any culture outside the walls of the compound. This is such a loss. Tourist resorts have sprung up catering only for the English, pubs selling British beer, British soaps beamed directly to bars to be watched during happy hour while munching on fish and chips.

A friend of my family was visiting Skiathos with his family last year. I received a call asking to visit us. After all, it's only a short boat ride to Pefki.

"Sure, I told him. Come and stay for a few days. You will love it."

The next day, he and his wife arrived. We greeted them at the gate and showed them to their room. They walked through the house into the garden, looked at me and asked.

"Where's the pool?"

"See that big blue thing over there? It's called the Aegean Sea. That's our pool," I told him.

"Sorry, we can't stay anywhere without a pool," he said.

Alex could see I was getting a little angry with these people and put a calming hand on my shoulder. Being a perfect host and full-blooded Greek, she was concerned that people coming to visit her were not satisfied.

In the genuine spirit of philoxenia, she made a call to the hotel next door and arranged a room for them next to the pool, and paid the bill.

We never saw them again.

Our village is hibernating for the winter.

Fields are cleared of fruit and vegetables. Bare earth has replaced the lush crops of giant green watermelons and ripe red tomatoes. Vines no longer need attention; they are busy regenerating themselves for the coming spring. We all need to sleep sometimes. Grapes have been picked. Wine is quietly fermenting in homes and *tavernas* all around the village. The residue of grapes left over from the wine pressing has been distilled into the local spirit, *tsipouro*. Olives are picked; some are stored in jars for garnishing Greek salads, but most have been pressed into golden virgin oil.

Most of the village restaurants have closed for the winter. The few still open cater to the locals. With no work to be done in the fields, farmers, fishermen, priests and the local doctor sit in front of warm log fires in village cafes, drinking their home-made *tsipouro*, chatting and playing backgammon. It's a time to unwind from the rigours of the year and recharge for the next.

Alex and I were looking for a restaurant for lunch. As we drove through the village, we saw that all of them were closed and dark. We were just about to try the next village, when we saw a flicker of flame from a fireplace through the window of a small fish *taverna* near the harbour.

As we entered, heat welcomed us from the log fire and the faint smell of cigarette smoke. Despite the "No Smoking" signs pasted to the windows, there were ashtrays on every table.

The restaurant was not busy, just a few tables occupied by the men of the village. Most waved or nodded as we took a table near the fire. This was no elaborate tourist restaurant. This was plain with bare walls, none of the normal paintings of Greek scenes. No pictures of boats normally found in fish *tavernas*. No, this was very basic and typically village-style. But it was clean and the people were friendly.

The owner came over, spread a paper tablecloth in front of us and placed a red tin jug of wine on the table with two glasses and a basket of bread.

"What would you like to eat?" asked the owner.

"What fish do you have?" Alex asked.

The owner spread his arms apart and put his head to one side in a sign of apology.

"Sorry, no fish today. The boats haven't been out, and I will not cook frozen fish."

"I have *pythakia*, (barbecued lamb cutlets) a special Greek salad with home-made feta and olive oil, fried cheese and fried courgettes, stuffed tomatoes or peppers, or pasta in the oven."

"Okay," Alex replied. "Let's have a salad, stuffed tomatoes, and we will try the lamb cutlets, but well done, please."

"No. I will not overcook my food. I will not present black cutlets to my guests. If you don't like them the way I cook them, have something else. You will thank me in the end."

Well, that told us.

I looked around the restaurant. The old men were sniggering. They knew this chap was proud of his cooking and was a temperamental chef. They were obviously waiting for the entertainment.

A while later, the food arrived. In this little,

dark dingy fish *taverna* with no fish, we had probably the best meal we had ever eaten in Greece.

Looks aren't everything.

I love living here.

Lunch on the hoof.

Today was cloudy and drizzly in our village, but being the last market day before Christmas, it was especially busy.

The lady selling village fire, *tsipouro,* in unmarked bottles was doing a roaring trade. I recognised a couple of *taverna* owners buying a few bottles. They seemed quite a bargain at only four euros for a 1.5 litre bottle, not a bad price for internal central heating. I often wondered why they would take the large bottles and decant them into miniatures before serving. In every *taverna*, there are always rows of these small bottles on the table. So I asked George, the restaurant owner, for the reason.

"It's so we can keep count of how much everyone is drinking," he told me.

By the look of the table in yesterday's *taverna*, I'm surprised they could even see the bottles, never mind count them.

The guy who sells honey has gone up-market for Christmas. He has put labels on his produce so we can tell if it's *pefka*, or oregano honey. We usually just buy a jar or two and hope for the best. We are never disappointed.

We bought a few chestnuts and some fresh fruit and wandered around until I saw a pickup truck with rabbits for sale. They seemed quite happy, with plenty of space, fresh straw and a bowl of food.

"Nice rabbits," I told the owner.

"Yes. My rabbits are delicious," he told me. "Add red wine and tomato sauce, but only a little garlic." He lifted his hand and formed a circle with his finger and thumb and kissed it to emphasise the taste.

These were not pet rabbits, they were ingredients.

I watched their little noses twitch and considered buying them all to let them run free in my garden, but Alex pulled me away.

"Look, this is a village," she told me. "You

can't save them all. It's the way it's always been done here. Don't judge."

This is the way of country people worldwide. I remember my aunt in Devon who bred lambs for the table. So Alex had a good point. But I did walk away feeling a little sorry for them.

We are off to lunch now. The *taverna* cats are expecting us and we would hate to disappoint them.

I'm not going to order rabbit though.

Today we economised.

When in Greece, because I love the food, I always order everything available. The local *taverna* owner sees us approach and always brings another table in anticipation. He knows the food would never fit on one table. Alex and I spend a lot of time in Athens and the UK, so miss the village food. We always make up for it when we are here. The *taverna* owner is happy, we are happy, and the cats are happy. Everybody wins.

But we have guests at the moment. My brother is here for Christmas. He is very much like me and appreciates the village food, but my mother is also with us. She is a little more prudent than us, and not used to excess.

"Peter, you order far too much food," she scolded. "We can't possibly eat all of that."

"But Mum, I want you to try everything."

Being proud of my Greek island village, I want her to experience the atmosphere and the wonderful tastes not available anywhere else in the world.

"You spend far too much money, and it's wasted, then you feed it to the cats," she complained. "Let's not go to a *taverna* tomorrow. Let's just have a pizza at home."

So, reluctantly, I agreed to forgo my normal over-ordering and cook a pizza.

This morning Alex and I went to the supermarket to buy the ingredients for a pizza.

First, I was getting low on wood for the bread oven, so on the way, we passed by the wood yard and ordered a truckload. Fifty euros spent.

At the supermarket, Alex spent twenty minutes at the deli counter. Pepperoni, six varieties of cheese, ham and assorted goodies. We needed flour and yeast for the pizza base, and more olive oil. While Alex was browsing the deli, I walked around the supermarket and somehow filled the trolley. Another two hundred euros.

On the way home, I remembered we

needed some wine, and the gas for the patio heater had run out. Another fifty euros.

We arrived home, fired up the bread oven. Spent an hour kneading bread for the pizza bases. Alex rushed around, setting the table. I rolled out the bases, added the tomato sauce, cheese and pepperoni, and put them in the bread oven. The oven was too hot, pizzas burned to a crisp in two minutes. So I let the heat die down a little, made more bread dough, spent another hour kneading, made more pizzas. This time, they were fine.

I gave my mother the first one from the oven. She took a bite.

"It's lovely but I'm not very hungry today," she said, and gave it to the cats.

So far today, I have spent three hundred euros for half a pizza.

Tomorrow, we are going to the *taverna*. I want three extra tables, everything on the menu, and lobster on the side.

I need to economise.

Greece always wins in the end.

It's a lovely day in our Greek village. The mountains across the Straits of Artemision are lit with bright sunshine. The recent wet weather has turned to snow on the peaks just in time to add a festive feel to the island.

Yesterday's wind and rain have not dampened our spirits. It's a good excuse to snuggle up in front of the log fire in the village *taverna*, drink a little local wine, share a *meze* of charcoal-grilled sardines, deep-fried squid and barbecued octopus. It's a day of relaxation and reflection.

We have family staying with us for Christmas. I watch as my brother, who used to consider anything more exotic than meat pie to be foreign food, is now chewing away at *calamari* and octopus while sipping *tsipouro*. A *bouzouki* strikes up in the restaurant's corner, and I watch as his feet tap. He is slowly adapting to Greek culture and loving it.

I have now been part of Greece for twenty-five years. Being married to Alex, my sparky Greek wife has been a life-changing experience.

In our early years in the UK, they weaned us on simple basic food. Although nourishing, it did lack the variety found in Mediterranean countries. When I was a kid, pasta came in tins, but only hoops. The fish variety was "Birds Eye", and they only had fingers. Garlic was unsociable, and we only found olive oil in pharmacies to pour into our ears, and never into salads.

When I married a Greek, all of this rapidly changed.

Alex realised this stuffy Englishman needed opening up. First on her list was to introduce me to the wide variety of Greek food, initially using shock tactics.

A tasty-looking fritter would appear on my plate in a *taverna*. When I couldn't place the taste, she smiled and told me I had just eaten sheep's testicles. The next dish turned out to be fried brains in batter. I soon lost my fear of the unknown and embraced all food offered.

My mother still needs a little work. We did a little shopping yesterday in the nearby market town, and sat in the square for a coffee. The waitress arrived. Alex ordered a large Greek coffee. I ordered my usual frappé.

"What would you like, Mum?" I asked.

"A cup of tea please."

To quickly explain. In Greece, tea is usually only drunk if you are poorly. So there is a large variety which is available from the pharmacy. The waitress adopted a sympathetic look, assuming her to be suffering from something. , and asked in a kind voice:

"What tea would you like?" she asked kindly. "Mountain tea is excellent for your chest, or we have raspberry, peach, sage or lemon."

"No, breakfast tea with milk, please," my mother replied.

This confused the poor girl. She had never heard of breakfast tea. I could see this was going nowhere, so ordered a cappuccino. Mother was not impressed.

Give her a few more days and she will be

drinking strong Greek coffee, *ouzo* and dancing the *sirtaki* with Alex ...

Greece always wins in the end.

I'm still not too keen on testicles though.

Greek music is the best.

Browse through the radio channels in Greece, and you will always find a choice of typical Greek village music. In some areas, you will struggle to find anything else. Greeks are proud of their heritage and love anything traditional. It's not the stereotypical tourist music of Zorba style *bouzouki*. No, it's the actual folk music with clarinet and traditional Greek bagpipe that looks like a goat with its legs sewn up. (It is actually a goat with its legs sewn up).

Nightclubs in Greece play the real traditional music with an Eastern flavour combined with more modern songs. We know these clubs as *bouzoukia*. They are expensive nightclubs with live music and dancing on the tables.

People buy trays of flowers and shower the performer with carnations if they like the performance.

As well as *bouzoukia*, there are other nightclubs known as *skilathika* (σκυλάδικα), otherwise known as "Dogs' Houses". These are more earthy and traditional. It's an authentic experience to visit either. Women get up on tables to dance freely. They encourage stage invasion to dance with the performers. You must join in and be part of the show. You will soon realise why traditional music is still popular.

But we can only find real Greek music in the villages. Sit in any local *taverna*. They will always have a radio or tape blaring out the proper stuff. Reedy voices accompanied by squeaky fiddles and clarinet. It's a lovely accompaniment to the warmth and atmosphere, which reminds you that real culture still lives in this wonderful country.

In England, we don't have that any more. I would love to bring back the old English music. Wouldn't it be nice to turn on the radio and find "Hey Nonny-Nonny" playing on a lute? Harpsichord music combined with harp melody.

You could watch live music shows of Morris men with bells around their ankles hitting each other with sticks. This would certainly catch on with the Friday night revellers in England's cities. It's already common to hit each other with sticks, just add a few bells, and go straight back to tradition.

Gone forever.

But in Greece, the tradition will never die.

Dancing in our village.

The *taverna* was quiet. The only sound was the crackle of the log fire, and the occasional click of worry beads being wound around an old man's wrist.

Then Alex arrived like a fresh breeze. All eyes turned to her as we took our seats.

"*Kalimera*," she yelled into the kitchen to wake up the sleepy cook. "*Ti fagitó écheis símera?*" (What food do you have today?)

A sleepy-looking man sauntered out of the kitchen, spread the tablecloth in front of us and recited the menu. We ordered our lunch and Alex stood up to walk around the restaurant, admiring the pictures on the wall and chatting with the old men.

She noticed one chap had a guitar case leaning against the wall beside him.

"Do you play?" she asked, pointing at the instrument.

"Yes, but it's only a hobby," the old man replied. "I'm not very good."

"Doesn't matter, we're all friends here. Let's hear it," Alex told him.

A group of old men on the next table woke up and clapped their hands in encouragement until the guitar player unzipped his case, strummed a few chords to tune up, then started playing an old Greek village song.

Our food arrived. We sent a jug of wine over to the old man playing the guitar and listened to the sweet music as we enjoyed our lunch.

The door opened, and a man walked in carrying a tom-tom. He sat next to the guitar player and tapped the drum in time with the music. Alex could resist no longer. She sprang to her feet and danced. The old men clapped as she performed a classical fisherman's dance in the middle of the previously sleepy *taverna*.

Soon, the cries of "Opa!" radiated around the room.

One man got to his feet and started to dance. Alex sat down and clapped in time to the rhythm. The *taverna* owner who had been watching the show with a smile, got up, rummaged in a cupboard and found his instrument. It was a goat with its legs sewn up, a *tsambouna*, Greek bagpipes. So, we had a band.

As the sun set, lunch became dinner. Families from the village had heard the music and streamed inside to join the fun. We arrived home after midnight, having left the party in full swing. But with more wonderful memories of our Greek village.

For Alex, this is normal. Wherever we go, she always has people dancing. Her spirit and love for life infect even the most formal-looking characters.

They always end up smiling in the end.

The Kallikantzari.

I n Greece, it's not just Santa who will sneak down your chimney, there are also some very unwelcome invaders who want nothing more than to cause as much misery as possible. These little trolls only come above ground during the Christmas period from 25 December to 6 January to wreak havoc on your lives.

After spending the year trying to destroy the world by sawing away at the Tree of Life, the *kallikantzari* emerge into the world looking for freshly baked Christmas goodies. Although they live on snakes, worms and frogs, they love sugar and that's why many housewives leave some sweets at different spots in the house in a vain attempt to make them act nicely.

They sneak into the house by climbing down chimneys, through keyholes and any windows foolishly left unlocked. They break furniture, steal food and announce their presence with creaking doors and bumps in the night, leaving food crumbs on the floors before they run away back underground as the cockerel crows.

They are small and most have a limp, or a lisp, or goats' hooves or elongated arms, with long nails and black tails.

According to legend, any child born during the twelve days of Christmas was in danger of transforming into a *kallikantzaros* during each Christmas season. To prevent this, babies are bound in tresses of garlic or straw, or you can singe the child's toenails.

According to another legend, anyone born on a Saturday could see and talk with the *kallikantzaroi*.

A large part of Greek Christmas and New Year's holiday traditions was in the past dedicated to keeping these goblins out of the house, away from the children, and away from the food.

The *kallikantzari* hate the sun. They also

hate fire, the cross and holy water, and have a very short attention span, so as hard as they try to do harm, they never succeed.

Sometimes an old shoe would be burned in the fireplace. The smell will keep them away. A handful of salt is thrown on the fire to crackle and fizz to scare away any lurking on the roof. A pig's jaw can be hung behind the door, but the best method was to leave a sieve in the house. Being dim and unintelligent, they would all gather to count the holes, as most of them could only count to two it kept them occupied until the sun came up, so they had to go back underground and wait for the next nightfall.

On 6 January, Greeks celebrate the "Blessing of the Waters", known as Epiphany Day, "God Emerging in the Light". Epiphany Day brings the holiday season to a close, sending a message of spiritual rejuvenation and inner cleansing. This is also the last day the *kallikantzari* have here on Earth. Intimidated by the light and love, Greece's Christmas trolls are driven back into the earth to axe away at the Tree of Life.

I think the moral of this story is that these creatures represent negative energy. They come during the darkest days of the year to test us when our guard is down. But, by wreaking havoc above ground for twelve days of the year, the Tree of Life has had a chance to grow back, thus saving the world for another year. They remind us it may be dark now, but it will be short-lived. The light is coming. Hang in there and all will be fine.

Merry Christmas From Peter and Alexandra.

Christmas Day.
SPIT-ROAST TURKEY AND SONGS OF PRAISE.

What a great Christmas Day in our Greek village!

Warm sunny weather with blue cloudless skies. With an outside barbecue, and wood oven, we just had to cook Christmas lunch outside.

Alex unwrapped the turkey while I lit the charcoal. When nice and hot, I threaded it onto the spit and set the motor turning. I threw a few logs into the bread oven to prepare for the trimmings and we sat in the sunshine listening to carols while sipping an ice-cold coffee. By early afternoon, everything was ready to serve. The table was set and food laid out, we sat down to enjoy a three-hour lunch with friends and family and local wine. It was perfect.

After lunch, I was happily snoozing in my favourite chair when the phone rang. Alex answered, it was our local *taverna*.

"Wait a moment, I'll ask him," I heard her say.

She put the phone to her chest.

"Do you want to go to the *taverna*?" she asked me.

"We have just finished a giant lunch. I can't eat another thing for days."

"Peter doesn't want to come," she told them.

I heard muffled talking from the phone while Alex nodded, then smiled.

"OK, we will be there," she said.

They had said the magic words: "There will be music."

Alex can never refuse a musical evening. Music means dancing. Her favourite thing in the world.

So, reluctantly, I eased myself out of my favourite chair, washed and dressed and we went to the *taverna*.

Nicos came out to greet us and led us inside. There was a table set up with soft drinks and nibbles, a few nuts, and sandwiches. Some people were wearing their best clothes, some men were wearing ties. I felt underdressed in my casual shirt and joggers, but nobody seemed to mind. As we sat at our table, two girls holding guitars squeezed behind a microphone. They had obviously been waiting for us to arrive before starting the evening.

Before playing, one girl smiled and called across to me, speaking in English, "Welcome Peter. I hope you enjoy our celebrations."

They started to play and people in the *taverna* clapped their hands in time with the music. But instead of yelling the usual "*Opa!*" they were shouting "Halleluiah" and "Amen".

It was a Christian revival meeting. We were there to celebrate the real meaning of Christmas.

The music was lovely, and the people were so friendly. That day, we really felt a part of the village and were honoured to be included in their private meeting. We got to feel the genuine message of Christmas through these lovely, smiling people in the village. By the time we left, we had made more lifelong friends.

Exploding pomegranates and cake on the ceiling.

Today we welcome the new year Greek style. The first job is to make the *Vasilopita* (Greek New Year's cake) served at midnight on New Year's Eve to celebrate the life of Saint Basil.

It's a job Alex and I always do together. We mix the ingredients into a large bowl and always cover ourselves with sticky cake mix, up to our elbows. Last year I had the brilliant idea of using a high-powered food mixer. This didn't go well. I set the food mixer too high and it covered us with most of the cake as it sprayed around the kitchen. Today we welcome the new year, Greek style. The first job is to make the *vasilopita* (Greek New Year's cake) served at midnight on New Year's Eve to celebrate the life of Saint Basil.

It's a job Alex and I always do together. We mix the ingredients into a large bowl and always cover ourselves with sticky cake mix, up to our elbows. Last year I had the brilliant idea of using a high-powered food mixer. This didn't go well. I set the food mixer too high and it covered us with most of the cake as it sprayed around the kitchen. We were scraping cake mix off the ceiling until Easter. So, this year it's sticky elbow time again.

After baking the *vasilopita* cake, we insert a coin through the base. When cut, we say the person who finds the coin is granted good luck for the rest of the year.

Next on the list is the New Year's food. The *meze,* or Greek appetiser dishes. Whether your party guests stay all night or just for a short time, you will need to feed them. Dishes such as stuffed grape leaves and *spanakopita* are perfect because you can leave them out for people to enjoy throughout the night.

Alex will dress up in her Santa outfit and empty the kitchen cupboards of anything that can make a noise. We then pile these up near the Christmas tree ready for when the time comes to bash them loudly together.

As midnight approaches, we begin the countdown. First, we turn on all the lights in the house to welcome the new year. Then all the taps in the house are turned on to let the water flow to ward off evil spirits.

As the clock chimes midnight, we run around the house and garden, clashing the pots and pans together, pour a glass of *ouzo* and toast the new year.

Then we take our ripe pomegranate and leave through the back door, walk around to the front of the house, then hurl the pomegranate onto the floor, which smashes and distributes the seed of abundance into the house.

Next comes the *podariko*: first foot. We join hands and step over the threshold, ensuring we lead with our right foot, and try not to slip on the pomegranate juice.

Alex and I wish you all a very happy, healthy and abundant new year. May all of your dreams come true, and your heart be filled with love and happiness.

Happy New Year from your friends in Greece.

A Note from the Author

I write about Greece. It doesn't take too much imagination. I just look out of the window and see the beauty of my subject spread around me. The bright Greek sunshine in an unreal blue sky. Orange and lemon trees swaying gently in the cool breeze. The sound of crickets. The perfume of mountain herbs invading my senses, the distant tinkle of bells tied to the collars of goats grazing happily on the hills.

Writers are a strange bunch. We isolate ourselves in closed rooms with only a keyboard for company. We rip out our souls and spend months and years obsessively perfecting our art.

Few of us will ever become rich, but this is not why we do it. We write for love.

The most incredible compliment any writer can get is to hear from you. It's such a wonderful experience to look online to see someone who I have never met has enjoyed my book and taken some of their valuable time to tell me.

If you have enjoyed my book, please let me know by spending a few moments to leave a review for *Musings from a Greek Village.*

Peter Barber, 2023

About the Author

Peter Barber was born in Watford, in the UK, and flits between Bedfordshire and Athens with his Greek wife. He spends as much time as possible in Greece messing about in boats, enjoying both the weather and the company, but mostly the food and wine.

Having nothing to do on a Greek island is time-consuming. When not amusing the locals by sinking his boat, Peter writes books.

The Parthenon series is a trilogy based on Greek life.

Peter's Books

The Parthenon series:

Book 1:
A Parthenon on our Roof
Book 2:
A Parthenon in Pefki
Book 3:
A Parthenon on our Roof Rack

Peter Barber's Musings:

Book 1:
Musings from a Greek Village

Contacts and Links

Email: peterbarberbooks@gmail.com
Website: https://peterbarberwriter.com/
Facebook: www.facebook.com/peter.barber.771/
Twitter: www.twitter.com/greekwriting

Writing About Greece

Join the Facebook community, Writing about Greece, a group founded by Peter Barber and his wife, Alex, dedicated to Greece and people who love Greece.

Or type Writing About Greece in the Facebook search box.

We Love Memoirs

Join Peter Barber and other memoir authors and readers in the **We Love Memoirs Facebook group**, the friendliest group on Facebook.

www.facebook.com/groups/welovememoirs/

Or type We Love Memoirs into the Facebook search box.

More Ant Press Books

AWESOME AUTHORS ~ AWESOME BOOKS

If you enjoyed this book, you may also enjoy these other Ant Press memoir series. All titles are available in ebook, paperback, hardback and large print editions from **Amazon**.

These two booksellers offer FREE delivery worldwide.
Blackwells.co.uk and **Wordery.com**

More Stores
Waterstones (Europe delivery), **Booktopia** (Australia), **Barnes & Noble** (USA), and all good bookstores.

PETER BARBER
Award-winning bestselling author

The Parthenon Series

1. A Parthenon on our Roof

2. A Parthenon in Pefki
3. A Parthenon on our Roof Rack

Peter Barber's Musings

1. Musings from a Greek Village

VICTORIA TWEAD
New York Times bestselling author

The Old Fools Series

1. Chickens, Mules and Two Old Fools
2. Two Old Fools ~ Olé!
3. Two Old Fools on a Camel
4. Two Old Fools in Spain Again
5. Two Old Fools in Turmoil
6. Two Old Fools Down Under
7. Two Old Fools Fair Dinkum

One Young Fool in Dorset (Prequel)
One Young Fool in South Africa (Prequel)

Dear Fran, Love Dulcie: Life and Death in the Hills and Hollows of Bygone Australia

BETH HASLAM

The Fat Dogs series

Fat Dogs and French Estates ~ Part I
Fat Dogs and French Estates ~ Part II
Fat Dogs and French Estates ~ Part III
Fat Dogs and French Estates ~ Part IV
Fat Dogs and French Estates ~ Part V
Fat Dogs and Welsh Estates ~ The Prequel

DIANE ELLIOTT

Lady Goatherder series

Butting Heads in Spain: Lady Goatherder 1
El Maestro: Lady Goatherder 2

EJ BAUER

The Someday Travels series

From Moulin Rouge to Gaudi's City
From Gaudi's City to Granada's Red Palace

From an Umbrian Farmhouse to Como's Quiet Shores

NICK ALBERT

Fresh Eggs and Dog Beds series

Fresh Eggs and Dog Beds: Living the Dream in Rural Ireland
Fresh Eggs and Dog Beds 2: Still Living the Dream in Rural Ireland
Fresh Eggs and Dog Beds 3: More Living the Dream in Rural Ireland
Fresh Eggs and Dog Beds 4: More Living the Dream in Rural Ireland

For more information about stockists, Ant Press titles or how to publish with Ant Press, please visit our website or contact us by email.

WEBSITE: www.antpress.org

EMAIL: admin@antpress.org

FACEBOOK: https://www.facebook.com/AntPress/

INSTAGRAM: https://instagram.com/publishwithantpress

www.ingramcontent.com/pod-product-compliance
Lightning Source LLC
Chambersburg PA
CBHW071257110526
44591CB00010B/702